9/6/06

A LIGHT THAT IS SHINING

A LIGHT THAT IS SHINING

An introduction to the Quakers

Harvey Gillman

QUAKER *Q* BOOKS

First edition published November 1988, reprinted 1991 and
1994. Second edition published February 1997.
This edition published January 2003 by Quaker Books
Reprinted 2005
Friends House, Euston Road, London NW1 2BJ

http://www.quaker.org.uk

© Harvey Gillman

ISBN 0 85245 346 9

Design & typesetting: Jonathan Sargent
Text typeface: Utopia 9.5/14 pt
Printed by Thanet Press Ltd.

PREFACE

This book is intended to introduce Quakers to people who, while they know little about them, would like to know more. Though it is my personal description of Quakers, I have tried to make it as objective as possible. The various drafts have been read by a number of Friends and a few friends who are not members of the Society. I am greatly indebted to them for their help and have tried to meet their points and adopt their suggestions wherever possible. This book is limited to the experience of Quakers in Britain and I have not attempted to write about those living in other parts of the world.

This new edition takes account of new structures and developing concerns. Quakers try to respond to the needs of the time. The hope is that changes are not brought about by fashionable theories or practices but are a response to the leadings of the Spirit, as we come to understand them.

Harvey Gillman

CONTENTS

INTRODUCTION

I once found myself at dinner with a group of people I scarcely knew. Over soup the conversation turned to employment. I admit I used to find it difficult discussing the job I had, that of Outreach Secretary for Quakers in Britain, because unlike being a teacher or a plumber, it means so little to most people. I said 'I work for the Quakers.' Silence followed. Several eyes fell upon the soup in front of them, or looked through the window. Well, what do you say? 'How nice', or 'Oh dear we shouldn't talk about religion' or 'They're good people, aren't they?' or 'Don't they spend a long time meditating in silence?' or the famous 'Wasn't Elizabeth Fry something to do with them?' Often it is simply a conversation stopper. The host or hostess may well sigh and think that a substitute should have been found for alcohol. 'You do drink orange juice, don't you?'

On that occasion, however, I was told that since it was not every day that they had a Quaker to dinner, I was to earn my food by telling the gathering what Quakers were all about. It was quite a challenge and I do not know just how much they understood. I do remember that I was still talking as the ice-cream found its way onto my plate.

*   *   *   *

In Britain and Ireland there are about 18,000 members of the Religious Society of Friends, as Quakers are officially called.

There are also some 9000 attenders, people who worship with Quakers but who have not (yet) taken membership. Around the world there are about 340,000 Quakers altogether, with large numbers in the United States, Latin America, and East Africa. Like most British Quakers I was not born into a Quaker family. I joined the Society in 1978 at the age of thirty. Five years later, I became Extension, now Outreach, Secretary of one of the departments based at Friends House, the central offices in London of Quakers living in England, Scotland and Wales. My particular brief was to describe Quaker convictions and beliefs to enquirers who for a number of different reasons wish to know more about them. The difficulty was how to describe this strange and, to me, very attractive group of individuals who hold a variety of differing beliefs and who use a whole range of differing words to describe their experiences. This is the dilemma of this introductory book. I shall try to convey the range of convictions, ways of worshipping, consequences of religious insights in the area of social concern, and the somewhat odd structure, from a point that is both personal and representative of the Society in Britain Yearly Meeting (that is England, Scotland and Wales) of which I am a member. It must be emphasised right from the beginning that for Quakers a general description of faith is likely to end up as the lowest common denominator of a number of differing points of view. So a personal statement may prove to be a way in to Quakerism rather than a barrier. At any rate I hope so.

A Native American chief who once sat in the quiet of a Quaker meeting for worship said through an interpreter that he loved to hear 'where words come from'. He loved to listen to the silence beyond the words, the silent meaning which words are often inadequate to express. I am conscious that words divide people, that one person's experience will lead to a rejection of words like 'God', or 'Christ', whereas another will feel that any reference to religious experience without them will be incomplete. Quakers believe that all people should listen to each other, to hear 'where words come from'. We need to bear in mind that all human beings are on a journey, that each journey is important, and that the attempts to describe what matters most to us are precisely the ones where we most often fail.

Religion and the Human Journey

The word 'religion' sets off alarm bells in the minds of many people. It may smack of enforced hymn-singing at school, boring Sundays when you were not allowed to do things you especially wanted to. Or else it may remind you of people you know or have met, who spend their time being pious and telling other people how they should live their lives. On the other hand, it may summon up for you an area of life you know little about, as fewer and fewer families and schools pass their religious tradition to new generations. A recent survey for instance showed that many teenagers could say very little about the festival of Easter; Christmas, of course, is known more widely and for the most part it has become an annual binge, quite separate from a religious calendar.

For those of us who were born into a particular religious tradition, religion may invoke also the joys of childhood, the times when we were happy and secure and our parents had the answers and the world had meaning. If anyone then questions us about our faith, we may feel attacked and also suspect that the questioner is finding fault with our background and our family. We become defensive and say that religion is a topic you do not talk about in public. For all these reasons and because so much harm has been and is being done in the name of religion throughout the world, it is necessary to look at what we mean by religious experience. I want to start, therefore, not with an institution, or a book, or a series of rules, but with human experience. This is where Quakers usually begin.

The Human Journey

Elizabeth Kübler-Ross, a counsellor and writer who specialises in work with the dying and the bereaved, has written:

> Every individual human being born on this earth has the capacity to become a unique and special person unlike any who has ever existed before or will ever exist again.[1]

It has been said that sex was the taboo subject of the nineteenth and early twentieth centuries. This is far from the case today. Until a few years ago death was the taboo subject that had replaced it for us moderns. A society like ours which places so much emphasis on living life to the full, which often means the sheer pursuit of pleasure and possessions, obviously fears anything that stands in the way of this pursuit. Besides, we have put those close to death out of the way, into hospitals, hospices, and homes for the aged. Yet counsellors, psychologists and social workers are beginning to realise that we have to look at our fears of death, to help us live life more deeply.

Until recently religion was also becoming a taboo subject. Scientific progress had become a god and talk of spirituality, mysticism, 'the search for something deeper' was regarded, outside of certain prescribed areas, as decidedly cranky. This has changed in the last few years, where people have grown suspicious of scientific experts, indeed of authority figures of most kinds. More and more people are searching and are not afraid to admit it, though the results are not always positive and creative, as the proliferation of new and sometimes authoritarian cults reveals.

A phrase much loved by Quakers and used frequently by George Fox (1624–1691), the great preacher of the early years, is that we need 'to answer that of God' in everyone. I have pondered over the meaning of that phrase ever since I joined Quakers. In the next chapter, I shall look at it in greater depth, but it seems to me that it is something to do with a creative power working in our lives to bring us to fulfilment, to an awareness of our worth, to a love for others and for God, however we define God. For a Quaker, religion is not an external activity, concerning a special 'holy' part of the self. It is an openness to the world in the here and now with the whole of the self. If this is not simply a pious commonplace, it must take into account the whole of our humanity: our attitudes to other human beings in our most intimate as well as social and political relationships. It must also take account of our life in the world around us, the way we live, the way we treat people who are different from ourselves, animals and the environment. In short, to put it in traditional language, there is no part of ourselves and of our relationships where God is not present.

Each of us is unique. The test of any religious community is how far all its members are cherished as unique individuals with talents to contribute to the life of the community. And how far this community also cares for people outside itself.

The English Quaker William Penn (1644–1718) was the founder of the once Quaker province of Pennsylvania in the now United States of America. His attempt to create a land of peace, harmony, and justice was a valiant effort to base a society on

Quaker convictions. This attempt was called the 'Holy Experiment'. In a sense, I believe that the Religious Society of Friends is such an experiment. Like many experiments, things go wrong, people are hurt, reality does not always live up to the ideal.

The attempt is made nevertheless to live out religion on a day-to-day basis and to respect the uniqueness and specialness of each person's experience. It is in this uniqueness that one can often see most clearly that power for love and creativity which is usually called God.

1

THE FOUNDATION:
God within the Heart

For much of their early history, Quakers suffered persecution, precisely for the courage they had in upholding their convictions in their everyday lives. Even the name 'Quaker' was first used in contempt. When in 1650 George Fox appeared before a judge on charges of blasphemy, he told the judge that he should 'tremble at the word of the Lord'. The judge then described Fox and his followers as 'Quakers'. The name has stuck, but the other title 'Friends' (originally Friends of the Truth) is the one most often used amongst Quakers today. Besides, it is very pleasant in a group to refer to co-seekers and co-finders as Friends, even if they are strangers. It can create a good atmosphere for the building of a community. The title 'Religious Society of Friends' first appeared at the end of the eighteenth century and is used by Quakers for business and legal purposes.

Quaker Convictions

You will not find the convictions of Quakers in this country set out in any creed. From early days they have stressed that their faith is something they live rather than put into particular words, and creeds can make simply for an outward conformity of belief. The formal creeds of the church as they have come down to us today were the results of the efforts of theologians to define what was true in opposition to the various 'heresies' current in several parts of Christendom. In this way orthodoxy (meaning right opinion) was established. Many who called themselves Christians were, through excommunication or even violence, cut off from the larger body for refusing to accept these verbal formulations of belief. The language in which the creeds were written was the language of the learned, often with the political support of the imperial authorities, so that many of the uneducated recited the creeds without understanding them.

I have already written that words are often divisive. The same words often mean different things to different people and similar ideas are sometimes expressed in very dissimilar ways. So when it comes to talking about basic beliefs, Quakers have a certain mistrust of theological terminology.

As William Penn wrote:

> …it is not opinion, or speculation, or notions of what is true,…that…makes a man a true believer, or a true Christian. But it is a conformity of mind and practice to the will of God, in all holiness of conversation [*behaviour*], according to the dictates of this divine principle of light and life in the soul.[2]

Early Quakers maintained that the church of New Testament times was composed of people who had a direct personal experience of what they described as God's saving power, and who acted out their lives accordingly. For these early Christians what mattered was experience not intellectual assent to doctrines. The Quaker pioneers believed that personal religious faith was of the same nature. They claimed that they were reviving primitive Christianity and that they too like their spiritual forebears were the children of God. They felt however that the other churches of their day had lost the spontaneous experience of God beneath age-old accretions of institutionalism, non-Biblical doctrines, and violent oppression of one group by another.

What then is the foundation of the Religious Society of Friends? I should put it this way: there is a creative, loving power in all people and in the world around. Many call it God, though it is beyond all names. Everyone can become aware of it directly by listening to its prompting in their hearts and in the hearts of others.

Quakers feel more able to become aware of this power in the silence of their meetings for worship. In the quiet, they maintain, the still, small voice can speak to them and direct their lives. The experience of quiet waiting upon God gives them strength to go back into the bustle of the world, the better to serve their fellows.

It is not in the institution of the church, nor in the hallowed pages of a book, that God is most keenly to be found, but in the human heart. For most Quakers, the model of this meeting with the divine and its transforming power in everyday life is Jesus of Nazareth, his life, his teaching, and his death and its empowering effect on others. The rest of this book is really a commentary on these convictions.

As human beings, we can all find fulfilment in our relationship with this power, whatever name we give to it. It gives meaning and purpose to our lives. It is our focus of unity. That it touches all parts of human existence leads Quakers to assert that life cannot be separated into categories of 'sacred' and 'secular'. Nor can we divide the world into compartments labelled 'religious', 'political', 'social' and so on. The way we act in every sphere depends greatly on what we believe about the nature of the world. John Woolman (1720–1772), an American Quaker whose profound religious convictions led him to the campaign to abolish slavery and to a compassionate concern for animals, saw the interconnectedness of all life and wrote in his Journal:

> to say we love God…and at the same time exercise cruelty toward the least creature moving by his life, or by life derived from him, was a contradiction in itself.

So the Quaker faith is a holistic one, taking all experience as its arena.

This openness to what Quakers call 'the leadings of the Spirit' is seen most evidently in the way Quakers worship, as will be described in the next chapter. Because Quakers believe that there is 'that of God' in everyone they have no special ordained ministry. They recognise that each worshipper has particular gifts and that all present have an important part to play. This has led to a belief in the equality of the sexes and within their meetings for worship women play an equal part with men. Although Quakers have always been influenced by contemporary prejudices, they have nevertheless made a progressive and positive impact in the field of women's rights.

The Light Within the Darkness

When trying to communicate the truths that you have discovered through your own experience, it is often easier to talk in images than to resort to intellectual theories. Jesus himself taught through parables which were images from the everyday experience of his listeners. He spoke of the seed and the lamp, the treasure and the sparrow. When in the seventeenth century Quakers studied the Bible they noticed how few of the big words of theology were ever used there. There is no mention there for example of the words 'trinity' or 'sacrament'. So, because they thought themselves to be direct inheritors of the early church, they refused to use these words to define their beliefs. However, one of the key words Quakers have always used is the word 'light', which they associated with the risen Christ in their hearts.

Light is a natural and beautiful image even in these days of neon and the hologram. It represents security, warmth, and knowledge. It also however has an opposite side. It is no friend to that part of ourselves we should like to keep hidden. We do not always want all our faults to be brought forth into the light of day. It would be false to human experience so to emphasise the light that we neglected the darkness.

In his journal, George Fox wrote of his own unhappy youth as being a struggle against depression and melancholia and a fervent longing for God. In a passage dated 1647 he spoke of his inward sufferings and his inability to understand why he had to undergo 'great temptations'. He wrote:

> And I cried to the Lord, saying 'why should I be thus, seeing I was never addicted to commit those evils?' And the Lord answered that it was needful I should have a sense of all conditions, how else should I speak to all conditions; and in this I saw the infinite love of God. I saw also that there was an ocean of darkness and death, but an infinite ocean of light and love, which flowed over the ocean of darkness.[3]

This passage points not to an empty optimism about the world, as if to say 'God's in his heaven. All's right with the world.' On the contrary, Fox, like other Christians, believed that suffering is part of the world's process, but that there is something greater than even the greatest suffering. There is a light which as John's Gospel has it (in the New English Bible version) 'shines on in the dark, and the darkness has never mastered it' and that light 'enlightens every man' (and woman).

Suffering

You are unlikely to come across the view among Quakers that there is a God in a heaven beyond death whose philosophy is 'a good dose of punishment never did anyone any harm and often does a lot of good'. Yet obviously suffering does exist. It is wrong to talk of suffering as always ennobling its victims and it does a great disservice to many who have suffered much to try to explain away its presence. The world is full of innocent victims and talk of sin as the cause of suffering has often in the past simply been a means of oppressing the powerless and keeping them in their place.

In his book *Night*, Elie Wiesel, the modern Jewish writer and Nobel Prize winner, wrote of his experiences of Auschwitz and Buchenwald. There is one particular harrowing incident which remains with me. Wiesel describes the death of a young boy in Auschwitz. A power station had been blown up by anti-Nazi saboteurs and the boy was to be executed for refusing to name the perpetrators. The inmates were assembled to watch the boy and two other prisoners die. Their necks were placed in nooses. The two adults to be murdered shouted 'Long live liberty!' Someone standing behind the author asked 'Where is God? Where is he?' The three victims were then hanged. The inmates had to watch the boy dying for more than half an hour.

Wiesel writes:

> Behind me, I heard the same man asking:
> 'Where is God now?'
> And I heard a voice within me answer him:
> 'Where is He? Here He is – He is hanging on this gallows...'[4]

I have often meditated on this incident. It has come to me while sitting in the silence of a meeting for worship as the ultimate question. The words are so ambiguous. Does Wiesel mean that his idea of God died the moment the boy died? In his novel *La Peste* (The Plague), Albert Camus likewise described the death of an innocent boy, this time through the plague. His conclusion was that he could not accept a God in a world where the innocent suffer. But Wiesel is much more ambiguous. As I re-read the passage and meditate on it, my faith leads me to believe in a God who suffers with the world, and is crucified and resurrected, as it were, in the thousand moments of our pains and joys. The question then is not so much why suffering exists. Multitudes of books have been written on that theme and they have persuaded very few people. The question is what do we do with suffering? George Fox in the passage from his journal has the telling phrase, 'I should have a sense of all conditions'. It is the wounded healer, the one who accepts the wounds, not passively but with a view to using them actively as a source of growth, and going out to help others with their wounds, that seems to me to be the model for the person of faith today. And it is not meant to be easy.

The Search

Quakers do not spend much time talking about sin. They tend to emphasise the good in people. The feeling of a lack of self-worth is strong enough in most people without 'preaching up sin' as early Quakers put it. But when we read many of the early journals (and it was the custom of Quakers to write journals instead of books of theology – personal experience over intellectual theories again), we can see a process of overcoming this sense of low self-worth. There is at first a feeling of inauthenticity, of life not lived fully or honestly; then there is a flicker of an ideal that life does have meaning. Sometimes this may come in a blinding flash, at other times as a result of a long period of perplexity.

The period of inauthenticity, of dullness, of alienation, is often described as a period of sin. But then gradually the individual feels that there is power working within which says 'No, you can't go on like this. Something has to change.' This is accompanied by an almost physical apprehension, a quaking even, or a nagging feeling that you have to take up your tent and move on. This struggle is in most of us a continuous one. At times we feel we have come through, made it to the light; at other times we feel, here we go again into the darkness. Isaac Penington (1616–1679) was a man who went from sect to sect, always discontented with what he found in each group. At last he became a Quaker. In his journal he writes:

> And indeed, at last, when my nature was almost spent, and the pit of despair was even closing its mouth upon me, mercy sprang, and deliverance came, and the Lord my God owned me, and sealed his love unto me, and light sprang within me.[5]

Even when he became a Quaker, there must have been moments when doubt took over again; and yet doubts and perplexities can be creative, for they also have a positive role to play in spiritual development.

The Directness of the Experience

Quakers do not believe this journey of spiritual growth is for a few exceptional people. It is one which all people are making at all times and in all places. As has already been mentioned, Quakers do not make a distinction between the sacred and the secular. This does not devalue the sacred but upgrades the secular.

Quakers share with other mystics the insight that God can be found in the everyday experience of all people. It is in the here and now that communion, real sharing, can occur. I have in the past stayed for short periods in monasteries for the quiet and peacefulness of the surroundings. I have noticed that if we think that we can escape from the world's problems by taking on a 'holy' life we are often much mistaken. The world is always with us even in the most set aside places. This is one of the deep insights of monastic life. One monastic tradition which I find very appealing is the law of hospitality: each guest is Christ at the door waiting to come in. At this point the Catholic and the Quaker traditions are very close, for the holy is part of ordinary experience, the guest and Christ are one, when seen with the eyes of faith and compassion.

Just as Quakers do not limit the service of God to certain times, or places, or people, so they do not have a set apart priesthood, nor a religious calendar of events. Nor do they have set hymns, and the meeting houses in which they worship are not consecrated. They do not have set sacraments such as water baptism and breaking of the bread. Following the Protestant move away from the hierarchical church of pre-Reformation Europe, Quakers took the idea of the priesthood of all believers to its extreme. Lewis Benson, the modern American student of George Fox, put it this way in his *George Fox's Message is Relevant*

Today, that Quakers taught:

> As he (Christ) teaches he can be known as prophet. As
> he forgives and intercedes he is known as priest…As he
> guides and watches over us he is known as shepherd.
> He can also be known as counsellor and leader and
> commander.[6]

If that is the case then there is no need for any specific person
to be designated prophet, priest, or church leader. Quakers
would say that if people are open to the power of love and light
in their lives then they will themselves become prophetic and
priestly, and will not need to follow an external authority of
church leaders. They will become empowered to find God in
their hearts and to serve other people.

Quakers and Christianity

No water baptism, no priests, no creeds, no religious festivals,
just how Christian then are Quakers? Quakers in Britain and
Ireland are members of Churches Together in Britain and
Ireland. Most churches are members through the acceptance
of a creed, but Quakers, not having a creed, are admitted by
member churches under a special clause. So we are seen to be
Christian by other churches. The problem is of course one of
meaning. According to a conservative evangelical definition, if
you do not accept the Bible as literally the true word of God, or
do not have faith in the redemption and atonement by Christ on
the cross, then you are not a Christian. This would exclude from
the Christian community many people, even in the more mainstream churches.

In his great work on Quakerism known as the *Apology*, Robert
Barclay (1648–1690), a Scottish aristocrat and Quaker theologian,

wrote of the church as a body consisting of those who were:

> obedient of the holy light and testimony of God in their
> hearts...There may be members therefore of this
> Catholic church both among heathens, Turks, Jews, and
> all the several sorts of Christians, men and women of
> integrity, and simplicity of heart.[7]

This definition is much more universal in its application than
the conservative definition and is based on a meeting with God
in the heart, a turning to the light within. However Quakers
define Christianity, and there are differences among them, they
all see it as making for an open, inclusive community. There are
a few who prefer not to use Christian language at all and even
maintain that they are Quaker, not Christian. Certainly very few
Quakers in Britain today would accept the conservative evangelical view. Most would say that for them the teachings and
life of Jesus of Nazareth were central to the picture they have of
God. For some Jesus is God in a trinitarian sense; for others he is
the supreme ethical teacher; for yet others he is the human
being who has reached his divine potential.

My own position is that all human beings have this potential
and that Jesus of Nazareth through his life, his teaching, his
death, shows me the way to God; but the more I read the Bible
the more I am convinced that Jesus the Jew did not aim to begin
a new religion. He seems to have wanted to liberate human
beings, to enable them to have a more personal and dynamic
relationship with God. In doing this he points back to Old Testament prophets such as Isaiah. At the same time he seems to
have realised that the path he was taking could be seen in terms
of the suffering servant which Isaiah himself describes. The suffering servant accepts upon his shoulders the pain of the world

even to his own death.

Modern Biblical scholarship also tends to stress that what was described by the early church is not so much the actual life of Jesus as the church's own interpretation of it during the years after the crucifixion. The New Testament is the recorded experience of those close to Jesus. Quakers believe the spirit that inspired the early church is still alive today and is not bound to any one religious tradition. Indeed when Barclay was describing the catholic church (that is, the church universal) he also mentioned that it included

> all,…of whatsoever nations, kindred, tongue or people,
> they be, though outwardly strangers and remote from
> those who profess Christ and Christianity in words.[8]

It is not the word or the labels but the heart and the commitment beneath them that count.

Many of the early opponents of Friends claimed that the Quakers denied Christ, the Bible, even God. To me, however, it seems that they were expanding the experience of God to include 'that of God in everyone', a sort of universalist Christianity. Today, Quakers would also claim that they acknowledged and respected the insights of many religious traditions and also the sincerity of spiritual seekers outside of all religious organisations. Truth cannot be restricted to human definitions. The Spirit is greater than any one cultural image of it.

Guidelines

A good introduction to the breadth of British Quaker experience and conviction is *Quaker faith & practice – the book of Christian discipline of the Yearly Meeting of the Religious Society of Friends (Quakers) in Britain*. The subtitle sounds formidable.

Discipline here has a particular sense: it refers to a common purpose and conviction. Discipleship might be a more accurate word.

The book is an anthology of writings from the earliest days of the Society to the present day. It is revised each generation in accordance with the Quaker belief in continuing revelation. Our understanding of truth is not static, new light is always being sought and often it is found.

The book opens with *Advices & Queries*, a series of questions and insights which are used both for personal reflection and for reading aloud during meeting for worship. The first advice provides a good introduction to Quaker thought:

> Take heed, dear Friends, to the promptings of love and truth in your hearts. Trust them as the leadings of God whose Light shows us our darkness and brings us to new life.[9]

Among the matters dealt with in this book are approaches to God, worship, structure, ways of conducting business, living faithfully today, close relationships, social responsibility, the peace testimony and the unity of creation. It is a work of inspiration, a masterpiece of the spiritual search.

2

WORSHIP:
A Quiet Waiting

On one never-to-be-forgotten Sunday morning, I found myself one of a small company of silent worshippers who were content to sit together without words, that each one might feel after and draw near to the Divine Presence, unhindered at least, if not helped, by any human utterance. Utterance I knew was free, should the words be given; and before the meeting was over, a sentence or two was uttered in great simplicity by an old and apparently untaught man, rising in his place amongst the rest of us. I did not pay much attention to the words he spoke and I have no recollection of their purport. My whole soul was filled with the unutterable peace of the undisturbed opportunity for communion with God, with the sense that at last I had found a place where I might, without the faintest suspicion of insincerity, join with others in simply seeking His presence. To sit in silence could at least pledge me to nothing; it might open to me (as it did that morning) the very gate of heaven.[10]

Caroline Stephen (1835–1909)

This passage, written almost one hundred years ago by Caroline Stephen, the aunt of the novelist Virginia Woolf, reflects the experience of many people when they attend their first Quaker meeting for worship. Many find it an experience like that of coming home after a long journey. Of course, it does not always work this way. Some people get little out of it, some are bored, others find it a peaceful, pleasant time but would not go further than that. Quakers have learned to be rather fearful of too strong emotions in worship which in the past have proved divisive and it would not be expected that a meeting for worship should leave the worshipper ecstatic. It could better be described as a quiet waiting on God. But there are moments like those Caroline Stephen described, when the worshippers may feel deeply and spiritually moved by an awareness of the divine. It can be a life-transforming experience.

One of the problems is the word 'worship' itself. It can sound like the bowing and scraping before some tyrannical master. In fact the word derives from the word 'worth'. It is the time Quakers give to finding worth in their lives. Here there are no hymns, no sermons, no set prayers. There is an hour of stillness, of inward prayer, contemplation, and reflection. Anyone who feels moved to do so, may speak out of his or her experience: this is called vocal ministry. Ministry in this sense is not a function of an individual but a gift that all may exercise. At the end of the hour, the worshippers shake hands and the meeting is over.

To someone looking in from the outside, nothing may appear to be happening. For the participant, however, it is a contemplative and meditative experience, and above all a corporate activity. At its best a Quaker meeting for worship is a fullness. The worshippers are filled with a deep feeling of the Presence among them. This may sometimes lead them to an assurance that, to use Mother Julian of Norwich's words, 'all will be well' (and this in spite of the difficulties and problems besetting the world around). Whereas in some forms of meditation, the devotee is led away from the world, in the Quaker meeting one is led back – it has been said, 'When worship ends, service begins'. Through worship the individual becomes part of a large community of worshippers who are friends in the widest sense.

The meeting for worship is a public event, to which anyone is welcome. In meeting everyone has a part to play; the visitor is welcomed, the regular attender is cherished, the member feels at home. Within the meeting for worship itself no distinction is made, all are part of the quiet waiting, all are free to speak or remain silent. This quiet waiting also forms part of the basis of the Quaker business meeting, known formally as 'meeting for worship for church affairs'. This will be discussed in Chapter Five.

Silence is precious and healing. As Caroline Stephen put it 'To sit in silence could at least pledge me to nothing'. One does not lose by undertaking the experience. On the contrary, in a civilisation like ours where little value is given to silence and to listening, a Quaker meeting can be very therapeutic. At one meeting I attended, one elderly woman used to fall asleep each Sunday. Far from being put out by this, the local Quakers told me that she found it very difficult to sleep at home and the meeting for worship was the only occasion when she could sleep properly. They were delighted that they had provided the opportunity for her to fall into a healing sleep.

A Visit to Meeting

The word 'meeting' needs some explanation. Firstly, a meeting is a place, as in 'Swansea Meeting'. Secondly it is the collective noun for the worshippers at a certain place, as in 'Westminster Meeting has decided to redecorate its kitchens'. Thirdly, it is the occasion at which the group meets for worship – in this case it is short for 'meeting for worship'. Quakers say 'I am going to meeting this morning' as other Christians would say 'I am going to church'.

Because Quakers are quite few in numbers and meeting houses are scattered it is often difficult to find them. If you had looked in the phone book you may have had to look for Friends, or Society of Friends, or Religious Society of Friends, or Quakers, and then you would not necessarily know who you were talking to. It could be the warden of the meeting house, or the resident Friend, or caretaker, the clerk, an elder, or an overseer (we will consider these terms later). So if you have succeeded in speaking to a Quaker or in finding a meeting house, you have performed no mean feat. This is not because they are trying to remain invisible, but because there are often so few Quakers or the meeting house is out of the way. Some local groups of Quakers may not be as publicly-conscious as they might be and this can make finding them more difficult.

So you have found the meeting house. Or it might be a room in a community centre, school, church hall or a private house. The building itself may be three hundred years old or brand new, but whatever its age, it will be simple and functional. When you go in, you may well be greeted at the door with a friendly handshake. You will find inside no religious symbolism: no statues, no crosses, no crucifix, no altar, no pulpit. In the entrance hall you may find people waiting to go in, reading pamphlets, studying lists of activities, handing each other notices to be read out after meeting has ended, or just chatting. Most meeting houses have libraries and pamphlet racks and you will be most welcome to take any leaflet that interests you. In some Meetings, if you are new, then the Friend who greets you at the door of the meeting room may hand you a leaflet called *Your First Time in a Quaker Meeting?* You may be grateful for this during the next hour, as an hour of silence may be a new experience for you and it is good to have something to read or hold to help you settle down.

The meeting for worship begins when the first person sits down in the silence. One advice beloved of Quakers from the *Advices & Queries* is 'Come faithfully to meeting for worship with heart and mind prepared'. This does not mean preparing a speech in advance. That would spoil the spontaneity of the worship. What it does mean is keeping meeting for worship and your fellow worshippers in your mind during the week so that the weekly meeting is not an addition to or a substitute for your prayer life, but an integral part of it. Some Quakers try to set apart a short period each day for silent contemplation as it is difficult trying to pack the whole of one's week's worship into one hour on Sunday morning. Coming with heart and mind prepared also means literally arriving on a Sunday in a relaxed state so that you can enter into the worship without difficulty. This is not always easy of course, if you have to see to the children, prepare the meal, or cover some distance to get to meeting. This intermingling of silence and daily life is found also in the silence before meals that many Quakers observe. The whole of life and all its activities become a sort of communion.

So into the meeting room. You will find a simple room with chairs or benches arranged in a square or a circle. In the centre is a table with a vase and flowers and usually copies of the Bible and *Quaker faith & practice*. You will see the worshippers in all sorts of postures, thoughtful, meditative, worried, looking out of the window, stroking their beards or clasping their beads, eyes closed, eyes open, all of them seated. Some may have adopted the hands-open-facing-upwards-on-the-knees posture which derives both from Buddhism and medieval Christian mysticism and is also used by some Christian charismatics. Whatever posture is natural to you is the one to adopt. Righteousness does not come from a bruised bottom and a strained shoulder.

When I go to meeting on Sunday I have a particular pattern that I sometimes follow. I sit down and watch the other people coming into the room. I often greet them with a smile or a slight nod of the head. After all, it is a society of friends and it is good actually to greet your friends when you see them. I may recite quietly to myself the 'Lord's Prayer' taking each phrase slowly, almost like a Buddhist mantra. I close my eyes and thoughts rise up from my life which demand my attention.

During the rest of the hour anything may happen. I may 'hold in the light' people who are going through a difficult time. I may even get to the point of stillness where I feel at one with the world and then I do not need words or thought at all. I may follow the words spoken by others and be led into an area I had not anticipated. I may be inspired by the sound of a bird outside or led into a voyage of inner discovery through the passing of an aeroplane overhead. It is the not knowing which so appeals to me. The fact is that I may be touched by the moment, touched into joy, sadness, even despair or radiance – all gifts of the Spirit. Sometimes, I am touched by nothing at all, enfolded by doubt or uncertainty. These are also necessary stages of vulnerability. Then the meeting will end as two appointed Friends, the elders, shake hands which is usually followed nowadays by a general shaking of hands by everyone present.

On Prayer and Distraction

Once I took part in a series of Ignatian exercises led by an Anglican priest. These exercises take their name from Ignatius of
Loyola, founder of the Roman Catholic Society of Jesus (Jesuits).
During these exercises, we were told that thoughts often arise in
a silence because we have been so busy during our week that we
have repressed certain things which now leap up to demand
consideration. It may be, it was suggested, that we had to pay
some attention to these thoughts and our worship was precisely
the time we could deal with them. The Quaker meeting for
worship is not a time just for holy reflections and for chasing
away the lower breeds of thought. In fact the more you try to
push away thoughts you do not want to think about, the more
they persist, rather like a bad tooth. Thomas Merton, the great
twentieth-century Trappist monk and writer, wrote that thoughts
were like birds. You could let them fly around your head, but you
need not let them build their nests there. So if a distracting
thought arises during meeting for worship, let it be for a short
time. We all have troubled thoughts at times; we are not saints,
just seekers.

Prayer

One of the questions which often worries newcomers and
established Quakers alike is that of prayer. What is prayer and
what do we do when we pray?

Isaac Penington described prayer as the 'breathing of the
child to the Father which begat it'. It may be described as a
human response to the world around; an awareness of ourselves, of others, of that power most of us call God, working in
the world, loving it, transforming it, and empowering us. The
problem is that we often think of prayers in the plural rather

than prayer in general. Prayers seem to be formulas, words we recite; prayer on the contrary is a state of awareness where words may not be necessary.

I once met a Benedictine monk who was interested in the Religious Society of Friends. His problem was that he was tired of the repetition of words. There is a Catholic form of spirituality which believes that prayer is like a boat and that we can sail upon the words, even when we feel we should prefer to remain in port. The words help us along. There is good insight in this. But there are times when weariness takes over. This monk and I agreed that it would be nice if there could be a sort of silent mass. After all, what are the ingredients of the mass? There is a general preparation and awareness of our shortcomings, prayers to the glory of God, ministry of the word, the creed, prayers on behalf of the world and the people, confession, sharing of the peace, the preparation of gifts and thanksgiving for them, prayers of consecration, communion and the dismissal. These are set out in particular prayers led by the priest on behalf of the congregation.

Yet, however formal all these may appear, they have their counterpart in everyday life. We prepare ourself for meeting, aware of how we have not lived up to our ideals during the week. We open ourselves up to the world of creation, often with no more than a 'thank you', just as in confession we may have been able to utter no more than 'I'm sorry, I've done it again'. We bring to mind the needs of our friends, problems in the world, we think of people who have meant much to us. Thinking lovingly is a form of prayer. Quakers do not recite creeds, even silent ones, but they are mindful of their basic convictions, their place in the world, and how the world might be made more holy by their actions and their love.

Ministry

The word 'ministry' is often heard among Quakers in a much broader sense than elsewhere. Ministry is service. Quakers form a community in which they each serve one another in a number of different ways. There is no hierarchy of ministry; no one function is holier than another. The Friend who stands at the door performs the service of welcoming the worshipper to the worship. For some people, especially newcomers or those who live alone and have lost or never had the intimacy of touch, this is a very important ministry. It can be an affirmation of their presence at a level much beyond that of words. There is the ministry of the one who has arranged the flowers on the centre table, a task often regarded as a humble one, but in fact these flowers may take on in the worship a symbolism of growth and new life. They are a witness to creation.

And there is the ministry of the word, when the worshipper is moved to stand up and to speak from his or her experience. This vocal ministry may take the form of a prayer, a Bible reading, a reading from other literature, or more commonly may arise from the experience of the speaker. The meeting for worship is a public event and the speaker need not be a member. It is the Spirit that is speaking through the words of the person who ministers, and the words are shared by everyone. Sometimes the meeting may be completely silent for an hour. It is not only the action or the word that counts – simply being there as a sharer is a service in itself.

The impulse to minister often seems to force itself upon the speaker and this may be accompanied by a quickening of the pulse. Indeed early Quakers were known for their trembling before God, but on the whole Quaker ministry today seems to be characterised more by its intensity than by outward signs of emotion though I have heard ministry forced out of one speaker through her tears. The sincerity that shines through shows that ministry has come from a deep place in the life of the speaker. This ministry does not interrupt the silence but acts as a sort of vocal counterpart or counterpoint. Thomas Kelly (1893–1941) was an American Quaker whose writings on spirituality have made an impact beyond the Quaker family. In his *The Gathered Meeting*, he wrote:

> Brevity, earnestness, sincerity – and frequently a lack of polish – characterise the best Quaker speaking. The words should rise like a shaggy crag upthrust from the surface of the silence, under the pressure of river power and yearning, contrition and wonder... They should not break the silence, but continue it.[11]

At times what is said in meeting may not seem to fit in with your personal thoughts or may even sound contradictory. The feeling in a Quaker meeting is such that one may even be able to accept the ministry of others without agreeing on an intellectual level. Loving another person does not always mean accepting fully what he or she is saying. Above all, a Quaker meeting is not a debating chamber. It is not a matter of simply exchanging ideas about the world, however profound these ideas may be. It is a focussing of concern about the world at a deeper level, an affirmation of relationship and community, and a reaching out towards that which is both beyond and within. Though the worshipper may come to meeting tired, peevish, reluctant (and sometimes even leave in a similar mood), worship is a declaration like that of the boy Samuel in the temple: 'Speak, for I am listening'.

Meeting for worship usually takes place on a Sunday but

there is no Quaker religious calendar. Early Friends' rejection of Christmas and Easter as set times of the year for example was for them an affirmation of the ever present birth, death, and resurrection of Christ in their hearts. Indeed many Quakers used to keep their shops open on established religious festivals as a witness to this fact. In the eyes of others however this was sometimes seen as a canny way of earning more money! Nowadays, although this remains the Quaker position, some Quaker Meetings do hold a meeting for worship on Christmas day and also have carol singing. Easter likewise is often a time of special reflection on the theme of death and resurrection.

So strong was the reluctance to accept a church calendar that one early group of Friends even refused to believe that one ought to plan meetings for worship at all. The practical side of Quakerism is very strong, however. Most Quakers worship on a Sunday morning (set time) in a meeting house (set place) but this is for reasons of convenience, not because Sunday is a holier day than the rest of the week. As public transport in some areas gets steadily worse, some groups may well find that Sunday is an impossible day to meet and they may choose another day. Some Meetings also hold meeting for worship during the week as well as on Sunday.

Children and Young People in Meeting

Children and young people are important members of the family of the Meeting. Some Meetings have many children and young people at different ages and different levels of development. Sometimes there may be two, three or even four groups of them meeting in various parts of the meeting house or even in the homes of worshippers. There are also a few elderly Meetings where younger people are rarely if ever seen, though it is in

these places that the worshippers are particularly delighted to
see them.

Many of the very young would have difficulty in remaining
for an hour in the silence of the meeting for worship. It is usual
for them to stay in meeting for the first ten or fifteen minutes or
to come in towards the end. In their own meeting, they may be
discussing Bible stories or Quaker traditions, using crafts, games
and other activities to develop their own understanding and
insights. They may also be weaving, helping to prepare the tea
or coffee that are offered to all the worshippers at the end of
meeting, or singing songs from *The Quaker Songbook*. The aim of
the children's or young people's meeting is to give its members
an awareness of being part of the community, a knowledge of its
spiritual traditions, and of having a positive role in the larger
community around them. At one Meeting I visited not long ago,
the children were learning to bake bread and to understand its
importance in the life of many different societies. It was an
introduction to problems of famine, to Biblical symbolism, as
well as being an enjoyable activity in itself.

In spite of their traditional reputation for dourness, Quakers
actually like enjoying themselves, and of course teaching is best
accomplished through fun. They do not indoctrinate their children but try to communicate something of the joy that they
themselves have found in their life together. In one Meeting, the
children put on a play about the life of Martin Luther King after
worship one Sunday morning. It was very well performed and
had been written by a member of the Meeting. It was a privilege
to realise that we were all learning through this performance,
learning of the life of the great black American leader, learning
of the sufferings of the blacks in the United States, learning of
how suffering could be overcome. We ended up by singing 'We

Shall Overcome'. We had been led in an act of worship by our children through joy and song.

Some older children prefer to stay in meeting with their parents and sometimes take part themselves in vocal ministry. At Young Friends' gatherings there are often experiments with different forms of worship, some silent, some more pro-grammed and including music. It would be a mistake to presume that silence only appeals to older age ranges; a number of young people have been drawn to the Society through the stillness of its worship.

It is always advisable to check with Meetings to find out what facilities are offered for younger people, as sometimes there are meetings for them once or twice a month only. At other Meet-ings there might be no official arrangements made for younger age ranges, but Friends there would be very pleased to arrange sessions for them.

Weddings

It may seem odd to include Quaker weddings in a chapter on worship, but the marriage ceremony among Quakers follows the same lines as the usual meeting for worship. It is a specially appointed meeting yet the Quaker hallmarks of simplicity, openness, and spontaneity are all present. The ceremony begins in silence. Towards the beginning of the meeting a Friend will stand to explain to newcomers and family guests the procedure which will follow. The bride and bridegroom stand when they feel ready, take each other by the hand and make their declara-tions. First one partner speaks: 'Friends, I take this friend (full name) to be my wife/husband, promising, through divine assis-tance (or 'with God's help') to be unto her/him a loving and faithful husband/wife, so long as we both on earth shall live.'

The other partner then makes a similar declaration. When the declarations have been made, the meeting continues with a period of silence. As in a usual meeting for worship, out of the silence vocal prayer or ministry may arise relating to the people being married.

After this, the couple sign the marriage certificate which is then witnessed by all those present. Later the Registering Officer, appointed by the local Monthly Meeting, reads the certificate. The couple also sign the Civil Register. Traditionally Quakers did not wear wedding rings but nowadays couples often choose to exchange rings. An increasing number of Quaker women retain their own family names as a sign of equality between the sexes. Although they are not described as weddings, there have also been one or two meetings for worship to bless the relationships of same-sex couples.

Sometimes the Quaker marriage procedure is used by people who are not Quakers. The decision to allow this is made by the Monthly Meeting (see Chapter Five). Usually one or both of the partners will have some association with Quakers and will be in sympathy with Quaker ideals. It is the role of the registering officer to ensure that applicants are familiar with the Quaker understanding of marriage and the way weddings are arranged according to Quaker convictions. In this case also, the meeting for worship is a public event.

Funerals and Memorial Meetings

Quakers do not have a corporate 'line' on life after death. If you take experience as the basis for knowledge, then few Quakers have had a return ticket to the beyond to describe what they have found! The range of views vary from a personal survival after death, through an impersonal 'all will be one', to views which border on 'I don't really believe there is anything, but I know love must continue in some way or another'. The emphasis is always on living life fully in the here and now, and leaving the rest to God. Ideas of eternal punishment and damnation have little part to play in Quaker thinking. Nor is the hope of life after death seen simply as a reward for virtue, or as a reward for a difficult life. So at a funeral or at a later memorial meeting, in thinking of someone who has just died, Quakers concentrate lovingly on the life of the late Friend.

The meeting for worship on this occasion has no set form apart from the usual meeting. It may be held at a graveside, the crematorium, or in the meeting house. It is a service of thanksgiving for the grace of God displayed in the life of the departed, with thoughts of comfort and sympathy for those left behind. For this reason, Quakers tend not to wear black. Even in death, however much the mourners grieve, it is for the gift of life and God's love that thanks be given. Thus these meetings, though serious, are not necessarily solemn and can often reach a great depth. For some people, they are their first experience of Quaker worship and at least one Friend now maintains that he joined the Society because of the way Quakers conducted their funerals.

3

ORIGINS AND DEVELOPMENT:
The Growth of the Quaker Outlook

This chapter needs only to be brief as there are several books published on Quaker history, perhaps among the best is John Punshon's *Portrait in Grey*. I have always found history fascinating but mainly for the parallels it draws with the present situation. Early Quakers saw their movement as 'primitive Christianity revived': they saw the parallel between their own seventeenth century and the first century when the church was expanding from Jerusalem outwards throughout the Roman Empire. British Quakers today have become more and more interested in their seventeenth-century origins as they have distanced themselves from the more narrow evangelical Quakerism of the nineteenth century.

What we at this period of our history find striking about early Quakers in the 1640s and 1650s is their emergence at a time of revolutionary change which was breaking down old ideas of a strictly defined social order. The Roman Catholic Church had long ceased to have any power in Britain, although it was still feared by the political establishment. There was conflict in the Church of England between its Puritan and Catholic wings. There were questions about the role of the bishops; about the role of women (in the Baptist, Quaker, and other Separatist communities women had an increasingly important place but it was later among Quakers alone, that women were fully accepted as having equal status in the worshipping group and so on. Faction begat faction, as each group tried to establish its own particular truth.

As well as being overtly theological in nature, these conflicts were political and social in the widest sense. The whole question of how society could best be governed for the benefit of everyone was being raised and many of the answers given were radical. As George Fox travelled up and down the country, he met with others who also had spent time seeking for a more intimate relationship with God. This search was taking them away from the mainstream churches, and was eventually to lead to the founding of what is now known as the Religious Society of Friends.

These men and women who later became Friends, brought with them ideas they had found in the varying factions they had come from, and for a period the Quaker movement was a much less coherent body than it later became. In today's world of rapid change with fewer than one quarter of the members of the Society born of Quaker parents, we can see a parallel. The challenge to modern Quakerism is a similar one: how today to fuse ex-Baptists, ex-Anglicans, ex-atheists, ex-Buddhists, ex-practising Jews, ex-so many things, into a united society (though not a uniform one).

The Seventeenth Century

In the seventeenth century it was George Fox who put his stamp on this emerging group. It would be a mistake however to equate a movement with one man, charismatic though he may have been. Throughout the north Midlands and the North West, groups had already set themselves apart from the mainstream churches. Many of them met in silence without priest or pastor. Many of them already had rejected outward sacraments and were waiting for a new spirituality. John Punshon puts it in this way in his chapter on the environment of the earliest Friends:

> The age of outward and formal religion was over. The age of scriptural bondage and sacramental symbolism was done. Worldly pride and ostentation were doomed. Power was draining away from the kingdoms of the world and into the restored kingdom of God, for Christ was here to teach his people himself.[12]

It was Fox with his administrative ability and Margaret Fell, who later became his wife, who were able to fuse these groups into a society which has survived, while most other religious groups originating at this time have died away. Yet the Quaker movement was not to be united easily. There were clashes of personality as well as of principles. James Nayler (1617–1660), whose enthusiasm and charisma sometimes led his followers to excess, clashed with Fox on a number of occasions. In the 1660s John Perrott, an Irish Friend from Waterford, protested against the increasing centralising of decision-making among Quakers and condemned the custom of removing hats when a Friend prayed aloud in meeting, and of shaking hands at the end of the meetings. This almost led to a schism, but in spite of these differences Quakers spread and grew and met greater persecution. Between 1650 and 1687, it has been estimated that 13,000 Friends were imprisoned, 198 were transported and 338 died in penal institutions or of wounds inflicted upon them while they were attending meeting.

Persecution did not cool the ardour of the men and women who left family and home to become 'publishers of Truth'. It is from this period that the Quaker custom of 'speaking truth to power' arises. In 1657 Mary Fisher (1623–1698), who had sailed to Massachusetts to witness for the truth, travelled to Constantinople to try to convince the Sultan. Others sought audience with the Pope and met with imprisonment or death at the hands of the Inquisition. But it was this revolutionary desire to publish the truth that God was immediately accessible to all human beings that eventually led to the founding in the seventeenth and eighteenth centuries of Quaker groups in centres throughout Europe, North America and the Caribbean.

The Eighteenth Century

Like most fervent movements, the Quaker movement began to lose something of its impetus as its founding members died. From being a movement to preach a new or regained truth it took on the characteristics of an inward-looking sect, handing down traditions and regulating the activities of its partisans. From being a revival of the true universal church, Friends now saw themselves as a remnant keeping precious their past insights. In the eighteenth and early nineteenth centuries they became a 'peculiar' people, suspicious of the outside world, wearing distinctive clothes, speaking a language full of distinctive jargon, addressing each other as 'thee' and 'thou', and although they still held public meetings now and again, very few newcomers were attracted to them.

But this introspection was not total and Friends were still concerned about conditions in the world around them. John Bellers (1654–1725), for instance, forms a link between the early persecutions and the subsequent period of retrenchment, yet he carried on the social witness of the first generation of Quakers with his schemes for the welfare of destitute children and in his writings he speaks of the 'labour of the poor being the mines of the rich'. His theories influenced later radicals such as Robert Owen and Karl Marx. Similarly John Woolman was one of the first in the Society to condemn slavery, urge economic boycotts, and to care about conditions aboard ship. He also prompted Friends to see the connection between the way they lived, the possessions they owned and the violence and oppression which were part of the economic and political institutions of their day.

The interest some Friends showed in the social conditions of their day was matched by the fascination of other Friends for the natural world. If helping other people was a sign of the Christian life, the exploration of nature was a sign of human appreciation of a divinely inspired universe and the Quaker contribution was considerable. John Fothergill (1712–1780) played a notable role in the medical world; as did Peter Collinson (1694–1768) in botany. Towards the end of the period, John Dalton (1766–1844) and William Allen (1770–1843) made great contributions to chemistry. One of the most important discoveries of the eighteenth century, the smelting of iron by using coke rather than charcoal, was made by Abraham Darby (1678–1717), at Coalbrookdale in Shropshire. This and other inventions at Coalbrookdale had great bearing on the growth of the Industrial Revolution.

The Nineteenth Century

Gradually as the nineteenth century advanced Quakers began to look outwards from the small world of their own denomination as they were more and more open to religious and social insights from other traditions. The outside world had already witnessed the Methodist movement of which Quakers at first were very suspicious and yet this movement went on to influence most of the churches in one way or another. Some Quakers by the end of the eighteenth century believed that their Society had become too complacent, too introspective, and like many in other churches felt the need for greater personal commitment. During this period, often described as the 'quietist' period of Quaker history, the Bible had been read in the home, but there was fear in the Society that too much reliance on it at worship would interfere with the still small voice in the heart. Under the impact of the evangelical movement and the teachings of the Quaker evangelical Joseph John Gurney (1788–1847) these dissatisfied Quakers turned again to the Bible. They felt that without Biblical and doctrinal authority they were powerless to overcome the world of sin and separation and came eventually to place a greater emphasis than did their immediate forebears on personal salvation and the doctrine of atonement.

In this they realised that they were close to Christians of other persuasions and this led them to cross the barriers of distrust and to work with others to improve society around them. Again William Allen was typical of this movement. His work with the Anti-Slavery Society and with the London poor reveals how Quakers were taking their religious convictions into the public arena and were beginning to co-operate with other churches. Similarly Joseph Lancaster (1778–1838), one of the first advocates of popular education on a national scale, drew other nonconformists into a society that later became the British and Foreign Schools Society. One of the best known of all Quakers, Elizabeth Fry (1780–1845), belonged to an old Quaker family, the Gurneys. She seems at first to have worn her membership of the Society quite lightly, but she was converted to a more evangelical faith and the fervour of this faith led her to prison visiting and then to prison reform.

There was however a backlash in more conservative Quaker circles who were afraid that such worldly activity and evangelical theology would dilute Quakerism. Eventually these conflicts led Quakers in North America to split up into different factions. Some of these divisions still remain, although gatherings are held to broaden mutual understanding of the different Quaker traditions. Even today the conferences are not always easy affairs when theology is discussed, yet there is much greater co-operation than previously.

There has always been a tension among Quakers between, on the one hand, the idea that the leadings of the light within were sufficient for spiritual fulfilment and, on the other hand, a reliance on the Bible and the atonement for sins through the crucifixion of Jesus of Nazareth. This tension was brought to the surface by the evangelical emphasis on scriptural authority and the perceived need for salvation, a position held by many prominent Quakers towards the middle of the nineteenth century. Later in the nineteenth century, the tension grew into conflict as among some Friends the growing belief in the scientific method was leading to a reassessment of the nature of authority and historical accuracy. Texts were being studied and questioned, and Biblical infallibility, a belief close to the hearts of many an evangelical according to which the Bible was literally true, was no longer being taken for granted. This led to three distinct trends among Quakers: the traditionalists or conservatives, who quietly relied upon the Light of Christ within; the evangelicals for whom the Bible was growing in importance as a source of authority; and the new modernists or liberals whose theology was suspect to both of the others as it questioned both the distinctiveness of some of the old customs and the literalness of the Bible. Under the impact of the new Biblical criticism and the work of Charles Darwin, the modernists were questioning their faith and were trying to see how the new knowledge fitted in with the old certainties. Whereas in the United States these trends resulted in splits, in Britain there has been no comparable division.

The Twentieth Century

There was no doubt that for many (often contradictory) reasons, groups of Quakers were confused about the direction their Society was taking. This search for a new direction and revival came to a head in a national conference held in Manchester in 1895. Under the leading of John Wilhelm Rowntree (1868–1905), Quakers saw the need for a greater commitment to an understanding of the origins of their Society, to a new teaching ministry (which eventually led to the creation of Woodbrooke College, the Quaker study centre in Birmingham), and to a new vision of the role of Quakers in the twentieth century.

This was on the whole a triumph for a more liberal, outward-going, emphasis but if it were a form of religious liberalism it was a liberalism enhanced by a mystical awareness of the presence of God. The notable exponent of this stream of Quakerism was the American, Rufus M. Jones (1863–1948). For him the personal experience of God is a mystical experience. In his *The Flowering of Mysticism*, he describes it thus: 'Mysticism is an immediate, intuitive, experimental knowledge of God, or one might say it is consciousness of a Beyond or of Transcendent Reality or of Divine Presence.'[13] The emphasis in this book is on the light within; less is placed on the historical crucifixion.

The last quarter of the twentieth century and the beginnings of the twenty-first century have brought about other transformations in the Society which I shall consider in Chapter Six. What is important about these different historical emphases in Quakerism is that to a varying extent they are all still alive today. There are still enthusiasts who wish to carry the message of George Fox to the market place; quietists who feel that too much outward activity gets in the way of the Spirit; evangelicals who witness to the effect in their lives of Jesus Christ, their saviour and redeemer; liberals whose gospel is a social one and whose emphasis is on a religious humanism; mystics who speak of the Spirit in all things; radicals who try to deconstruct the nature of religious experience, and others who would simply call themselves Christians, for whom no other title quite fits their understanding of religion. Indeed it is one of the joys, though not unmixed sometimes with anxiety, to have all these Quakers sitting down together in worship. For it is worship which brings Quakers together. And it is out of worship that arises the Quaker idea of service in the world.

4

FROM CONVICTION TO PRACTICE:
Faith into Action

> A body dies when it is separated from the spirit, and
> in the same way faith is dead if it is separated from
> good deeds.
>
> *The letter of James* 2:26

Their religious convictions and worship do not lead Quakers away from the world but lead them back into it to look for the Spirit working there. There are two words which Quakers often use to describe the practical work which flows from their spiritual insights: concern and testimony.

Concern

We often hear that people are concerned about particular matters: people are concerned about their children's future, nuclear energy, additives in food, the future of southern Africa, violence on television and so forth. They may not do much if anything about these matters, but they are worried and bothered. The word 'concern' has a more powerful meaning among Quakers. It refers to a religious compulsion to act in a certain way based on a 'leading of the Spirit'. Early Quakers left home and family under a concern to preach the truth as they saw it, just as Mary Fisher had a concern to speak to the Sultan or Elizabeth Fry to improve the condition of prisoners in Newgate prison. Similarly one could say that John Woolman had a concern about the possession and selling of slaves and felt compelled to act according to the dictates of the light within him. He brought this matter up time and time again as he travelled widely among fellow Quakers. It took quite some time before the whole Religious Society of Friends accepted his insight. Eventually however Quakers became the first group as a body to speak out against the whole institution of slavery.

These concerns, originally rising out of the experience of individual Quakers, were brought before the worshipping group to which he or she belonged. This is still the accepted procedure. The concern is thus put into focus, refined as it were, in a corporate search for the guidance of God and the group can then offer moral, spiritual, or financial support. Sometimes the group does not support the concern. It may ask the concerned Friend for further information or to reflect more deeply on the matter. Though the process may often seem slow and ponderous, it has enabled many Quakers to act wisely and faithfully in situations of uncertainty and even of danger.

I have often been quite impressed at how, by a sensitive listening to one another, Quakers have come to decisions which no one could have predicted at the outset. All this may take time, but that in itself is a good discipline. When it works well, everyone present can feel that they have been fully respected and listened to. Being part of the decision-making process, they can then support all the more the plans for carrying out the decision.

Testimony

'The very existence of the Religious Society of Friends may be seen as a testimony to the spontaneity of the relationship between human beings and God. It is a warning against institutionalism and the confinement of the human spirit.' It was not a Quaker who said that to me but the former abbot of an Anglican monastery.

The word 'testimony' is used by Quakers to describe a witness to the living truth within the human heart as it is acted out in everyday life. It is not a form of words, but a way of life based on the realisation that there is that of God in everybody, that all human beings are equal, that all life is interconnected. It is affirmative but may lead to action that runs counter to certain practices currently accepted in society at large. Hence a pro-peace stance may become an anti-war protest, and a witness to the sacredness of human life may lead to protests against capital punishment. The testimonies reflect the corporate beliefs of the Society, however much individual Quakers may interpret them differently according to their own light. They are not optional extras, but fruits that grow from the very tree of faith. As early Friends would have put it, they are the outward sign of a restored relationship with God.

Although it is for the peace testimony that Friends are best known, this is only one aspect of living according to the dictates of truth. It was precisely obedience to truth as they understood it that led Quakers to act in ways which others thought odd and even provocative. In 1659 Thomas Ellwood, a young Oxfordshire squire, was going about his business in Oxford when he met a group of his old friends who greeted him according to the courteous practices of the time. He stood there silently while his friends continued bowing, scraping, and taking off their hats. Finally they realised that a change had come over him:

> they were amazed, and looked first one upon another,
> then upon me, and then one upon another again for a
> while, without a word speaking. At length, the surgeon
> …clapping his hands, in a familiar way, upon my shoul-
> der, and smiling on me, said, 'What! Tom, a Quaker?'[14]

And Tom had not said a word! His whole manner of being would have told his friends that here was someone who did not treat others in an affected way, someone for whom the putting off of hats was an important matter (Quakers took off their hat for God alone in prayer), someone for whom words were important and not to be used lightly. Thomas Ellwood would have worn simple clothes, have used 'thee' and 'thou' and would have refused to address people by their titles. In a court of law he would not have taken an oath, for as well as the Biblical commandment against swearing, and for letting your 'yea be yea and your nay be nay', there was the belief that all your words should be truthful and swearing an oath suggested two levels of truth. So your behaviour and language were your testimony to the equality of all people and to the need for truthfulness.

Of course as social customs change so the testimony to simplicity and integrity needs to be expressed in more relevant ways. It is hard to have a concern about 'hat honour' when most people do not wear hats and you cannot withhold tithes when a tenth of your income or produce does not go to the parish. But what about paying that proportion of taxes which goes towards military expenditure? What about ways of living that have detrimental effects on the environment? Those are issues which are exercising a number of Friends today.

Nowadays Quakers no longer use 'thee' and 'thou' but are aware of the way they use language, especially recognising the need for gender-free terminology. It has even been suggested that the modern equivalent of the old plain speech is inclusive language, where one does not presume the masculine form includes the feminine. An example of this might be the use of 'people' or 'humanity' instead of the forms 'man' or 'mankind'.

The testimony against titles still holds. Quakers call each other by their first names and family names, irrespective of age, material or social status. Many also omit titles when communicating with non-Quakers.

Integrity and Stewardship

To some the Quaker insistence on integrity, simplicity and truthfulness may seem off-putting and puritanical. To others it may seem hopelessly idealistic. Yet to others it is proof of a commitment to spiritual values. It has to be stressed that these are the guidelines for everyday living rather than a description of it. In other words, Quakers are human beings with frailties like everyone else. Yet it is a fact that Quakers do have a sense of justice and honesty and are as a group quite idealistic. It is also part of their idea of testimony that their rejection of conventional approaches to a number of issues may well lead to suffering or simply to a reputation for impractical 'do-goodery'. They often feel able to act as they do because they feel that somehow and somewhere in the complexities of everyday life, God is working with them and through them.

It may be one of life's ironies that integrity also pays. Looking at the rather anti-materialist stance of many modern Quakers, it is sometimes surprising to reflect that a number of large businesses were actually Quaker in origin and became successful because people could trust the company to be honest and faithful in its business dealings. Indeed it may be said that Quakers were largely responsible for the establishment of fixed-price trading. Barclay's Bank, though no longer Quaker, grew in this way, as did Lloyd's. Similarly, the Friends' Provident Insurance was founded early in the nineteenth century and became one of the big insurance groups, but is now out of Quaker control.

When fortunes were amassed, the idea of responsible stewardship grew among the wealthy Quaker families, leading for example to the bettering of housing conditions for their workers. George Cadbury (1839–1922), a chocolate manufacturer, was also an adult school teacher, and he was keenly aware of the poor housing conditions of industrial workers. He founded Bournville Village which in turn influenced first the Garden City movement and then the planning of the post-Second World War new towns. Conditions in his factory were in the vanguard of enlightened industrial relations. The Cadbury and the Rowntree families, as well as the families of other Quaker industrialists, set up trusts which give much practical support to groups, both Quaker and non-Quaker, whose interests lie in the creation of a more just and enlightened society.

On the other hand, the connections between the misuse of the earth's resources, economic exploitation and violence have been emphasised by Quakers as far back as John Woolman in his 'A Plea for the Poor':

> Oh, that we who declare against wars, and acknowledge
> our trust to be in God only, may walk in the light...may
> we look upon our treasures and the furniture of our
> houses, and the garments in which we array ourselves,
> and try whether the seeds of war have any nourishment
> in these, our possessions.[15]

This link is made today by Quakers looking at how the world

economy is distorted by the vast expenditure on nuclear and other weapons, how much of the world suffers malnutrition, poor water supplies, hunger and drought, while fortunes are spent on non-useful commodities and armaments.

On a more humble level, the Quaker concern for the right ordering of the world's resources influences the way they use their own finances. Betting and gambling for example are very rare among Quakers and you will not find meetings organising raffles for funds. The principle here is one of using resources creatively and not gaining by other people's losses. This is particularly urgent today when many valuable social projects are dependent on money raised by the National Lottery. Quakers have spoken out against this form of national gambling and no Quaker project would accept money from it.

Moderation

> In view of the evil harm done by the use of alcohol, tobacco and other habit-forming drugs, consider whether you should limit your use of them or whether you should refrain from them altogether. Remember that any use of alcohol or drugs may impair judgement and place both the user and others in danger.[16]

So reads part of the *Advices*. You will note here that rules are not being set down. Some Quakers are teetotal, some drink in moderation. Some smoke, some refrain from all tobacco. The question is always: are you in control of your life, are you using your money wisely and creatively, are you setting an example to those over whom you have some influence? In this matter as in many others, it is easy to be carried away by social pressure and it is often hard to stick to principles.

Peace

A testimony is a lived experience, not a form of words. Often when talking about the peace testimony, Quakers refer to two extracts from George Fox from 1651 and 1661 which suggest that this experience was neatly formulated from the early days. The first statement by Fox was a refusal to take up a captaincy in Cromwell's army which was offered to him by Commonwealth Commissioners:

> I told them I lived in the virtue of that life and power that took away the occasion of all wars…I told them I was come into the covenant of peace which was before wars and strife were.[17]

The second statement is part of a letter signed by a dozen prominent Quakers to Charles II dissociating Quakers from the uprising of the Fifth Monarchy Men and trying to prove to the King that Quakers should not be punished along with this other dissident body. The extract usually quoted begins:

> We utterly deny all outward wars and strife and fighting with outward weapons, for any end or under any pretence whatsoever.[18]

Yet to quote these two documents out of their context is rather misleading. There was a wide diversity among early Quakers about the nature of 'the peaceable kingdom'. Indeed in Scotland and Ireland, it was in the Commonwealth army garrisons that Quaker ideas spread most rapidly, and many Quakers left the army at first for refusing to take an oath rather than for refusing to fight. It was only gradually that a realisation took place that fighting was incompatible with Christian principles. This was not a once and for all revelation; neither is the peace testimony today a static creed among Quakers. It is often a hard-fought inner battle and doubt remains over its consequences in the minds of many individuals.

There is no doubt that early Quakers' refusal to fight with outward weapons did not mean that conflict was to be avoided. Conflict was a part of life. If you wished to 'turn the world upside down' and bring it to a realisation that Christ was alive and God immediately accessible to all, then you would inevitably come into conflict with the authorities. But the weapons were those of truth and love, not the sword and fire.

In the eighteenth and nineteenth centuries, in the area now covered by Britain Yearly Meeting, the peace testimony was mainly a matter of making representation to government against particular wars, helping with relief work, and a refusal to rejoice at times of victory. Some Quakers were also active in organisations devoted to the furtherance of peace. It was not however something that affected the lives of most Quakers directly, just as warfare on the whole did not affect the majority of the population. Quakers aimed at living peaceably with their neighbours but being at peace for most of them was an extension of being part of the quiet in the land, minding one's own business, getting on with simple lives of integrity and where possible giving their leisure to philanthropy and adult education. In North America however the situation was different. Quaker settlers played a part in trying to mediate between the native Americans and the colonial settlers, often at great danger from both sides. They were also troubled by having to pay taxes to support a militia for the defence of settlements. In Pennsylvania, this conflict cost them the backing of the majority of the rest of the population and led them to abdicate power in the mid-eighteenth century.

The last hundred years have forced Quakers to look more closely at the whole nature and meaning of peace and at objections to war on grounds of conscience. The First World War saw large Quaker meetings in a number of prisons, when many of them refused to have anything to do with fighting whatsoever. Others took a relativist line and worked in the Friends Ambulance Unit or the Friends War Victims Relief Committee. One or two Quakers did enlist believing that it was a just war. Some of these were disowned from the Society for taking this stance, but this was not universal. Indeed these three approaches are the ways in which Quakers do react to fighting: the absolutist who refuses to have anything to do with war; the relativist who, while condemning the fighting, tries to mitigate the consequences of it; the small minority who enlist because they feel that their principles lead them to take up arms against an evil greater than warfare itself. It must be stated however that the corporate witness of Quakers is to the evil of all warfare as being against the will of God, who is a God of peace.

However peace is not simply the absence of war; it is a vision of human wholeness. It is the ideal of human beings finding fulfilment as individuals at personal, social and international levels. The many Quakers involved in counselling and marriage guidance today are a witness to the fact that reconciliation between people is part of the peace testimony. This principle also underlies the work of the Quaker offices in New York and Geneva which represent Quaker views to the United Nations, and the office in Brussels which presents Quaker views to the Council of Europe and the European Union. Bringing together estranged partners, bringing together diplomats from apparently opposing nations, bringing together opposing social groups and hostile minorities are aspects of the comprehensive

Quaker concept of peace.

During the last few years, some Quakers have been led to consider the need for non-violent direct action, to examine how much their finances actually pay for armaments, to consider how feminist thinking can liberate men from the need to work out their insecurities on the battlefield and to view the peace testimony as going beyond the human race to include the whole of creation. The beginning of the new century is a fruitful and exciting period in the history of the Quaker witness to peace, made more immediate by the dire threat hanging over the world in the shape of the nuclear bomb and environmental disaster. The challenge is greater than ever, but Quakers believe that God is involved in this challenge.

Reconciliation

The demands of justice often seem opposed to the need for reconciliation. What passes for peace may really be the silence of the oppressed. It would be too easy to dismiss Quaker concerns as simplistic or not grounded in the real world. The Quaker attitude is not one of keeping hands clean and saying 'we'll have nothing to do with this evil'. It is often a matter of being involved in negotiations before violence breaks out.

Quaker internationalism has led to support for international bodies such as the old League of Nations and the United Nations of today. It is here that Quakers feel many international disputes could be resolved without recourse to violence. Quakers sometimes act as mediators, receiving the confidence of opposing sides as in the Nigerian-Biafran war and the negotiations for the foundation of modern Zimbabwe. They have also been involved in the relief work after warfare has ended, as in France, Germany and Eastern Europe after both World Wars. In more recent times they have worked among members of mutually suspicious communities as in Sri Lanka and the former Yugoslavia. In working to remove the seeds of war and trying to help alleviate the mess brought about by warfare, Quakers have seen the connection between warfare and injustice, and realise that peace is often a slow process and needs constant vigilance. It was for their work in this sphere that the British Friends Service Council, together with the American Friends Service Committee, were awarded the Nobel Peace Prize in 1947.

Economic and Social Justice

This religious/political idea has forced Quakers to look at the whole of society and to consider the relationship between ideals and practice. At the present time there is a revival in concern about our social testimony and its radical implications for action. A number of Quakers are involved in politics in one way or another as a practical consequence of their religious convictions, though it must be pointed out that quite a few other Quakers have certain suspicions about too great an involvement in party politics.

This concern for social justice may be summed up in one of the *Advices*:

> Seek to understand the causes of injustice, social unrest and fear. Are you working to bring about a just and compassionate society which allows everyone to develop their capacities and fosters the desire to serve?[19]

At a time when unemployment is becoming the way of life for many and alienation grows apace, Quakers are considering the whole concept of 'work' and some Meetings and groups are beginning to sponsor projects for unemployed people. In east

London for example Quaker Social Action works in areas of great poverty and need in housing projects for the homeless and furniture provision for households in need; in Bognor Regis Quakers have also been involved in getting short stay accommodation for homeless people.

The injustice felt by large sections of the community is compounded by racism and prejudice against ethnic and other minorities. One recent Quaker poster announces that 'In Human Diversity lies the Creativity of God' and yet, for many people, diversity is threatening and increases insecurity. Questions of inclusivity, respect for people needing asylum from persecution, and for people of other cultures and religions face Quakers (and indeed all citizens) with the need for a more caring and equitable society. Hence the need today to proclaim with great vigour the message that there is that of God in everyone and that each individual has worth irrespective of colour, race, religion, sex, and occupation (paid or unpaid).

Penal Reform

In the early days of persecution, thousands of Quakers were jailed and hundreds died in prison. More recently many went to prison as conscientious objectors. Today, some Quakers face prison again as they protest against arms bases and taxation for weapons of mass destruction. This has given them some knowledge of prison life and a desire to reform conditions. Elizabeth Fry for example spent much of her time campaigning for literacy, privacy and better clothing for the women of Newgate prison and prisoners in general. Many a time she waited with women soon to be hanged, trying to console them in their last hours.

Throughout their history Quakers have campaigned against capital punishment as a denial of God's power to work in every man and woman. The emphasis today is on work with offenders in the probation and other services and on trying to find them a place in the community. Writing to prisoners on death row, being a human contact at a time of great distress is another way Quakers try to bring light into the darkness.

Education and Social Responsibility

Education is a matter of bringing out the potential of the individual and fostering an openness to experience. Quakers have long seen how important this process is and they are engaged in all aspects of the educational system. The majority of Quaker teachers work in state schools, but some teach in the eight schools run by the Society in England, most of which are co-educational. (Most of the pupils and teachers however are not Quakers.) In these schools the academic side of life is respected but it is the development of the whole personality which is the main goal. This includes the encouragement of artistic and practical skills. Many Quakers have also been involved in running progressive schools because they felt that certain aspects of education were not provided for elsewhere.

Woodbrooke in Birmingham is an international Quaker centre for adult education. It is residential and offers courses on a wide range of issues covering Quaker, Christian, interfaith, social and international studies. A number of Quaker meeting houses also serve as adult education centres and are used by a variety of organisations for educational purposes.

To respond to the concerns of individual Quakers up and down the country, committees and groups have been set up to study, for example, the social implications of housing and unemployment, economic, racial and criminal justice, environmental change, and truth and integrity in public affairs.

Thus the practical approach is based on study, analysis and experience. The kingdom of heaven grows from hard work as well as inspiration!

Work Abroad

Some years ago I travelled round southern Africa visiting various Quaker projects. I noticed then one or two significant characteristics of this sort of work. The main aim was to respect the dignity and independence of the people with whom Quakers are working. In these projects, the Quakers and their representatives were not acting as traditional missionaries, but rather as partners with an emphasis on sharing and helping people to help themselves. At the time there was an agricultural centre near Bulawayo in southern Zimbabwe. The Quakers involved were trying out simple forms of technology which did not rely on foreign spare parts and which could therefore be replaced easily. In addition to this, new plants were being introduced into the area to supply better sources of nutrition. A school had been opened and the workers were spending a lot of their time taking the new ideas into the rural areas to help the surrounding villages.

I found the same caring in a different project further south in Botswana, where refugees from countries with differing regimes had come together to escape oppression at home and to carry on with their education. As this refugee centre was situated in a village outside the capital, it was necessary to reconcile the differing perceptions of the villagers with those of the refugees, whom they distrusted. Education, help for the oppressed, and reconciliation, three traditional areas of Quaker concern, were fused in a comparatively small but vital enterprise. The centre has changed its emphasis and is no longer run by Quakers but the Quaker ethos persists.

The projects have changed over the years and the emphasis has moved from relief work to supporting small-scale enterprises, where people can help themselves and regain their dignity. Other schemes run, sponsored, or funded by Quakers as part of the national work or as concerns furthered by individuals or local groups, are educational, agricultural or medical in emphasis. British Quakers and their representatives have been working in several countries in Africa, Asia, Latin America and the Middle East as well as closer to home in mainland Europe. Often the Quaker presence is small and limited, but it is a witness to the need for peace and justice, and the respect due to all human beings.

Building Bridges of Co-operation

Quaker work camps began after the First World War. The main aims were reconciliation through reconstruction. In later years the projects have tended to last for one to three weeks, with half the group coming from Britain and the other half from the mainland of Europe and sometimes beyond; a few volunteers are Quakers, but most are not. The Quaker witness to bridge-building and care for the community is maintained in a very practical way and the work that is undertaken is work that otherwise might not be done. Over the years many international friendships have been built up as people have got to know each other while working positively for local communities. Recently the co-ordination has been taken on by an independent organisation, Quaker Voluntary Action.

5

QUAKER ORGANISATION:
Meetings and meetings

New religious movements often claim to be reviving old truths hidden under the dead weight of tradition. They create new structures to help them better to live out these truths in their new communities. But after a few years the founders die out and the next generation receives the wisdom second-hand and takes for granted the structures which the old pioneers struggled to evolve. As the movement loses some of its dynamism, the members rely more and more on organisation to carry them through. Soon these very structures are seen to be getting in the way of true life and a new movement comes into being to reform them.

This has happened among Quakers, yet the Religious Society of Friends has survived because it has had wise administrators and a structure based on the needs of its members from its early days. It is the paradox of practical mysticism.

This chapter is an attempt to introduce Britain Yearly Meeting from the point of view of its organisation. It is a simplification and it takes years before Quakers themselves fully understand its nature. My work in Friends House, London, brought me into contact with many committees whose names range from the obviously named Committee for Racial Equality to the more obscure Six Weeks Meeting Committee (which deals with the premises of London meeting houses). The trouble is often that as soon as one has understood one set of names, the committees seem to change their names or cease to function or amalgamate!

Meetings in Britain

Britain Yearly Meeting covers England, Scotland and Wales, with the Isle of Man and the Channel Islands. Within this there are about 490 local meetings, most of which are formally called Preparative Meetings. These form larger units known as Monthly Meetings, of which there are seventy-three. Monthly Meetings are part of yet larger units called General Meetings. There are nineteen of these.

Preparative Meetings (so called because they prepare business for the Monthly Meeting) may vary in size. Some may have fewer than ten, others as many as 200 members – and in addition they usually have a number of attenders attached to them. As there are no clergy, all members have a responsibility for the life of the Meeting, but each Preparative Meeting will have a Clerk, and most will also have Elders, Overseers and a Treasurer and a few committees to help them carry out their responsibilities.

The Monthly Meeting is the primary business meeting of the Society. Here membership is decided upon, so that when an attender becomes a Quaker she or he is accepted into membership by the local Monthly Meeting. The Monthly Meeting is also the body responsible for, amongst other things, the right and regular holding of meetings for worship in its constituent Preparative Meetings, the appointment of Elders and Overseers, the maintenance of a register of members, and applications for membership. It also has responsibility for the supervision of weddings and funerals, and the appointment of prison ministers, hospital visitors and representatives to various other organisations.

The Clerk and the Business Meeting

Every Preparative Meeting has its Clerk. The Clerk of the Meeting usually reads the notices at the end of meeting for worship. He or she presides over the business meetings and serves as a sort of combined chairperson and secretary. The business the Preparative Meeting might discuss is varied. It could be whether to make a donation to a particular charity or what activities to pursue in the local community. The meeting might consider the needs of the premises, whether to organise an exhibition in the town to make Quakers better known or how to write to the local Member of Parliament about an issue which is worrying the Meeting.

Quaker business meetings at Preparative, Monthly or Yearly Meeting level are held in the context of worship. They may take place after meeting for worship on a Sunday or at any other convenient time during the week. Attenders may join in as well with the permission of the Clerk of the Meeting. The aim of the business meeting is to discover the will of God. It is not a matter of bowing to the will of majorities or minorities, and Quakers do not vote: rather it is an exercise of listening to God through what each person says.

The Clerk discerns 'the sense of the meeting' and writes a minute which must receive, there and then, the assent, spoken or tacit, of the meeting. Do not be surprised to hear the Quaker phrase 'hope so' or 'I hope so' intoned by one or two experienced Friends present. They are saying that they hope the minute will be acceptable to the meeting. If no sense of the meeting is discerned, no decision will be taken, and no minute will be made except to record that the meeting is not ready to proceed.

Elders and Overseers

Elders and Overseers, of whom there will usually be several in each Meeting, are appointed by Monthly Meeting. These appointments are made usually for a three-year period. The most visible role the elders have in meeting is for two of them to shake hands to signal the end of meeting for worship. They have a particular responsibility for the spiritual life of the Meeting. This may mean organising Bible study, discussion groups and meetings for newcomers and other outreach work – in short, the education of the whole meeting, including children.

Overseers have more of a pastoral responsibility for the members and attenders. They give advice and information about application for membership and help with any personal difficulties that the worshippers may be encountering. They also keep in touch with people who cannot attend regularly or who are rarely ever seen at meeting, though they are members.

Both these roles call for great sensitivity as they are the practical implementation of the Quaker conviction that there is divine potential in everyone which needs nurturing and fostering. In a number of Meetings, people are appointed to a dual role of elder/overseer; in one or two places the roles have been abolished because it is considered that everybody is responsible. However the matter is dealt with, a real community is one based on worship and shows itself in caring.

General Meetings

The main purpose of the General Meeting which meets up to three times a year is 'for conference and inspiration, and for a broad oversight of the life and witness of the Society within its area'. Here there is much less emphasis on business and more on discussion of topics of general interest to the Society.

The General Meeting area may cover a large part of the country. For example Western General Meeting covers an area from Aberystwyth to Shrewsbury in the north and Milford Haven to Cirencester in the south. Quakers are used to travelling for conferences and meeting each other, but poor rural transport and difficulties for the elderly often prevent some people from attending. Recently the Meeting of Friends in Wales has been founded to take account of the need for a Welsh entity. However the problem of accessibility remains here as elsewhere. Scottish Friends have their own general meeting and again distances are vast and meetings scattered. Experiments are taking place in various areas to make sure that agendas and speakers are interesting enough to attract a whole range of members and attenders.

It must be emphasised that Quakers realise people have many different calls on their time and there is no compulsion or pressure to attend all these meetings. At some periods in their lives people are freer than at others. There is however a commitment on the part of members to help when and as they can.

Yearly Meeting

In the nineteenth century, one (undeclared) function of Yearly Meeting was to bring together young Quakers with a view to matrimony! I am sure that in one or two cases it may still have this function but Yearly Meeting as an annual gathering of up to eighteen hundred Quakers is still quite an event. Any business that needs a corporate decision is discussed at the large sessions and at its best the involvement of so many people in decision-making is a wonder to behold.

In addition to decision-making sessions, Yearly Meeting has in recent years considered more general questions such as international relations, racism, worship and our social testimony, our caring for the planet and its resources, the spiritual depth of the Society, the right holding of business meetings, simplicity and homelessness, and the role of young people in the Society. However fellowship is important and Quakers do actually enjoy themselves at these occasions, meeting old friends and making new ones. In recent years they have felt freer to celebrate the moving of the Spirit among them in song, dance, and drama as well as in the more traditional ways.

Meeting for Sufferings and Friends House

Of course there are difficulties when so many people are involved. Policy items which need a quicker response are resolved by the Yearly Meeting's standing executive committee known as Meeting for Sufferings. The name derives from the recording by this committee in the seventeenth-century of the sufferings and persecutions of Quakers for their religious convictions. 'Sufferings', as it is generally known in the Society of Friends, meets eight to ten times a year at Friends House in London and has representatives from each Monthly Meeting.

Friends House contains also the central offices of Britain Yearly Meeting and its library. The staff here are responsible to Meeting for Sufferings. The Recording Clerk's office oversees their work and services both Meeting for Sufferings and Yearly Meeting. The departments carrying out the central work of the Yearly Meeting are Quaker Peace & Social Witness, which is responsible for work abroad as well as for peace activities at home and abroad; for penal reform, community relations, homes for the aged, education and other aspects of social affairs; Quaker Life which coordinates religious education within the Society from 'cradle to grave', children and young people's activities, and racial equality and oversees the work of various Quaker centres. Communications Department deals with fundraising, sends out information about the national work of the Society to members and attenders, produces *Quaker news*, oversees posters. It has very recently taken outreach work with enquirers under its wing and the oversight of publication of literature to nurture the spiritual life of the Society. The Quaker Bookshop is open to the general public and stocks a wide range of Quaker and other religious material. There are also departments for the service of the premises, personnel, and finance.

Information about any of these can be obtained from Friends House, 173 Euston Road, London NW1 2BJ; telephone: 020 7663 1000. The website is www.quaker.org.uk

6

QUAKERS TODAY:
Respect for Diversity

Yearly Meeting for me is the time when Quaker diversity is at its most obvious. It is also the time when the search for unity, which is often called the search for the will of God, is at its most intense. Quakers are individualists who yet believe that unity is possible at a deep level. This is not unity of belief, certainly not uniformity of experience, but a unity in the Spirit. Paradoxically this unity is possible because it is based upon recognition of difference. Respect for 'that of God' in the other is the key factor. Diversity is seen to be a source of creativity, though sometimes it can be a challenge.

Once I attended a residential Yearly Meeting attended by over two thousand Quakers. This was the largest ever gathering of Britain Yearly Meeting. Some of the more introverted Quakers were a little apprehensive but the friendly mixture of bustle and silence satisfied most of them. Important decisions were taken such as on the role of Quakers within the Christian tradition – after lively contributions concerning the wording of the text, a Quaker response to the Baptism, Eucharist, and Ministry report of the World Council of Churches was approved.

There was also at this Yearly Meeting a presentation on the

role of women and their oppression in society in general, sessions on human rights at home and abroad, on human relationships and sexuality; there was a peace vigil and a celebration which took up all the themes of the week's activities.

In addition to the main sessions were held smaller gatherings devoted to particular issues and concerns of groups of Quakers. I attended on this occasion an introduction to various Quaker informal groups. There was the Friends Inter-Faith group which, now under the wing of the Quaker Committee for Christian & Interfaith Relations, organises meetings between representatives of different religions; the New Foundation Fellowship which considers the life and writings of George Fox, and sees them as a model for a renewal of an energetic Christian Quakerism for today; the Open Letter Movement and the Seekers' Association which aim through literature to challenge modern Quakerism to explore creatively contemporary thinking in philosophy, psychology, and theology. Also present were the Quaker Universalists who emphasise that all religious traditions are valid ways to God; representatives of the Young Friends Central Committee (now Young Friends General Meeting), a loosely constituted organisation most of whose members are in the eighteen to thirty age-range (liberally interpreted!) and which act as a vital link between many of the younger members and attenders of the Society; and the Quaker Socialist Society, which while non-party-political, sees the work for democratic socialism as a vital aspect of its members' Quaker faith. And this was simply an introduction to the twenty or so groups in the Society.

The Diversity of Friends

Friends come together as women, healers, Esperantists, historians, teachers, homosexuals, teetotallers, vegetarians, campers,

artists, world citizens, land value reformers, medics, and criminal justice reformers, amongst others. In fact I sometimes feel
that if there is an interest, some Friend has set up a group for it.
Recent years have seen the birth of new groups concerned with
sexual abuse, genetic engineering, ecology, and the promotion
of quiet retreats. But to be a Quaker does not mean that you have
to join yet another group or committee. The fact is that many
Quakers do like being with similar-minded people, but many
others enjoy attending meeting for worship on a Sunday and
cannot or do not wish to spend time on these other activities.

The Society today is quite different from what it was a
hundred, fifty or even twenty-five years ago. Social pressures
have been felt by Quakers as by everyone else. Today, as in probably no other period of their history since the seventeenth
century, most Quakers were not born into the Society but joined
as adults. Hence there has been a subtle change in the ethos of
the Society. There is a greater openness to the world around and
its culture and probably a loss of knowledge about Quaker traditions and ways of doing things. On the other hand there is a
growing awareness of the need for renewal. Society at large is
experiencing a hunger for spiritual values in reaction to the
growth of materialistic attitudes. It is out of this hunger that
many enquirers turn to the Religious Society of Friends and it
must be admitted that Quakers are not always able to respond
to this hunger. They tend to be tentative in the expression of
their beliefs, and are concerned not to force them onto others,
but this often seems like a lack of enthusiasm.

There is a growing awareness today among Quakers of the
need to deepen and broaden the witness for peace; to see how
the exploitation of our planet, the oppression of minority
groups and of women (who in fact constitute a majority), the

destruction of many species of animal, the reliance on fuels which may have dangerous consequences for whole communities and societies (expressed in the preoccupations of Quaker Green Concern), are all part of human alienation and result from a lack of the vision that all creation is of God and to be cherished as such. I see these issues as the ones that are to the fore in contemporary Quakerism.

With this goes the respect for the diversity of all people and of life-styles. The Society today reflects social trends prevalent in society at large. Unemployment and divorce have both made inroads into modern Quaker families and one-parent families and alternative ways of living are much more widespread than in former years.

The stigma attached to divorce, to separation, to being homosexual, is much less common and indeed in recent years the Quaker Lesbian and Gay Fellowship has done much to support homosexual Quakers and attenders. Not all Quakers have been able to overcome prejudice, but then few human beings can admit to being totally open to groups they have difficulty in understanding or of whom they have had perhaps little or no experience. Having written this, it has been my experience among Quakers that the vast majority have an openness to that of God in everyone to a degree that I have not found elsewhere. The chapter on relationships in *Quaker faith & practice* is a model of positive thinking on this and similar issues.

Young Friends

One of the trends in recent years that has worried many Quakers and indeed other churches is the disappearance of younger people from meeting. As adolescence draws on, religion seems to become boring to many people, however open that religion may be. Indeed it may be said that one of the problems of younger Quakers is that their parents are often so liberal that they do not provide the resistance that young people like to rebel against.

One of the more recent developments in the Society is the formation of 'Link Groups'. These link up young people over the age of twelve from a wide area for social gatherings as well as more serious day events and residential weekends. These groups try out experimental forms of worship and discuss topics which are raised by the young people themselves.

Quaker Life, through its Youth Officers, offers support, resources and training events, both at local and national level, to encourage and develop work with young people. It also organises the annual, national, four-day conference for sixteen to eighteen year old young Friends – Junior Yearly Meeting – where the leadership roles are taken by young people themselves. This renewal of life and liveliness among these young people is reflected also in the Leaveners, the Quaker Youth Theatre, whose dramatic productions have generated a great spirit of fellowship and fun in its participants and have brought the themes of spiritual depth and the need for celebration before the Society as a whole.

Young Friends General Meeting, mentioned earlier, also provides an important support group for people in the eighteen to thirty age range. It organises national gatherings, appeals, and local discussion groups and is often the means of enabling younger Friends, attenders and sympathisers to play a full role in the national life of the Society. Indeed it is through the inspiration that they have found at gatherings that a number of younger people have made their way into the Society.

7

BEING PART OF A COMMUNITY:
Membership and Commitment

If you go to meeting you will be hard pressed to tell who is the Friend and who the attender. (It really troubles me when I hear people saying 'I'm only an attender', no one is 'only' anything.) If there is no spiritual distinction between member and attender, the question is asked, why have membership at all?

Membership

Among the early Friends membership was seen as commitment to the promptings of the voice of Christ or the inward light as expressed in daily life. The universalist tendency among many Quakers, which stresses that all religions are illuminated with God's light, has led some to assert that there is no point in identifying too closely with one particular group. Quakers today would not dream of saying that truth was alive only among Friends. To become a Quaker is not a matter of saying here alone is all truth. It is to say: 'This is where I as an individual feel at home. Here I can worship in a way that leads me to fulfilment. Here I can find others who share my seeking and my finding. This is my community.' It is not a matter of being 'good enough' or 'intelligent enough', or even having this or that exact view about Jesus of Nazareth. It is a matter of believing that the relationship between the self, the community, and God are best expressed for you among these people. This is not to say that this relationship cannot be expressed elsewhere; a number of Quakers do worship in other places as well as in the meeting house. Membership does not lead Quakers to live only in the Quaker compound, as it were, but is a matter of making a public witness to the truth as they see it.

George Gorman, in his *Introducing Quakers*, states this well:

> Membership of the Society is not a mere formality, but is the outward sign of a truly personal involvement with a group of people who share common convictions about the meaning and purpose of life. These arise from the still centre of their being and in their sense of identity with others when they are open to them in loving relationships…Their involvement in this turns them out again to the wider community.[20]

Functional Membership

There are functional as well as spiritual reasons for formal membership. Quakers have to decide matters for themselves and carry out these decisions on a whole range of issues. Any such group needs people who publicly commit themselves to the work and to be responsible for it. Long before formal membership got off the ground, Quaker committees were set up to consider any matters that confronted the Quaker community. By becoming Quakers today new members are saying that, if they have the time and energy, they will agree to take on responsibility for a certain aspect of Quaker life. Circumstances change and they may be able to do today what was impossible yesterday, and vice versa. Formal membership indicates at least a willingness to consider such duties. Certain Meetings that I know are unwilling to ask attenders to take on responsibilities, because they feel this might be an imposition on them. Other Meetings on the other hand have to do so as there may be far more attenders than members and it seems that the attenders appreciate taking on these responsibilities.

One of the responsibilities is the financial one. Quakers give what they can and giving can always be altered according to circumstances. There is, of course, no subscription fee, but just as the decisions taken within the Society are the decisions of its members, so the work carried out by the Society has to be paid for by them. Each meeting has a treasurer who will advise the member on his or her contribution. Unemployment and domestic difficulties hit Quakers like everyone else and it is recognised that some people will be able to offer more than others. Many members pay by covenant which enables the Society to benefit from tax relief.

These responsibilities often extend beyond the local Meeting. Because Quakers are so small a body it is often quite easy to know many of the extended Quaker family beyond regional boundaries. My own job working with enquirers made it important for me to know that there was a group of committed Quakers in various areas to whom to refer new enquirers. Thus the members in that area act as the visible representatives of Quakers and are making a witness to Quaker insights and ways of living. So membership becomes not only a commitment to the group but a witness to society at large. This does not mean that you become a walking encyclopaedia of the highways and byways of Quaker theology and folklore, nor an example of outstanding virtue and righteousness. It does mean that you are saying that Quakers are still alive and (pacifically) kicking and have a viewpoint that is very worth stating and that you wish to be associated with them formally.

From Enquirer to Friend

We all remain enquirers for most of our lives. The journey stops at death and then probably only changes direction. But in Quaker jargon an 'enquirer' is someone who is new to the Society and possibly has only once or twice ever visited a Meeting, if at all. A 'visitor' is someone who is a newcomer to meeting or a member of another Meeting.

Most people who come to meeting do so because they have met a Quaker or have read some introductory literature. The journey to the Religious Society of Friends can be a long, complicated and circuitous one. It is often with trepidation that the newcomer crosses the threshold of a meeting house. This may be the first and only visit or else the first of many. It is when it feels right and the attender has the feeling of being at home that he or she may feel the desire or need actually to join.

Getting to Know More

Enthusiasm is fine, but being a member is rather like a marriage. There may be the shyness or the flirtation, the infatuation, the going steady, but the marriage begins over the coffee-cups and the newspaper when the ceremony is over. It is only right that both partners get to know each other well to avoid disillusionment. It is advisable to attend over a period of time to become familiar with the Meeting. In this way enquirers will get to know the community and have the time to ask all those questions that they felt they could not ask when they first went to meeting. New questions crop up all the time. Not everyone in the Meeting knows the answer. It is a bit like tourists in London asking the way to St. Paul's. Sometimes the answer is 'I'm new myself' or 'the best person to ask is so-and-so'.

Secondly, it is useful to bear in mind that you do not join the local Meeting but the Monthly Meeting; in a sense you join the whole society. So get to know as much of it as you can, by going to several different meetings for worship. Each Meeting has a different feel to it. If you live in a large city it is of course easier to visit several different Meetings than in other places, but on holiday you may well find there is a Meeting in the town and a visit will probably be well worthwhile.

If further help is needed before joining, you could contact an Elder or Overseer of the Meeting or else borrow some books from the meeting house library. Friends House in London will be delighted to provide any information needed and a visit to the Quaker Bookshop or the Library will provide you with many valuable resources.

Quaker monthly is published with enquirers particularly in mind. Weekend enquirers' gatherings are held at Charney Manor, a beautiful medieval manor house southwest of Oxford. Weekend and one day gatherings are also held in other centres around the country both by the Outreach Section at Friends House and by local meetings.

Application for Membership

Quakers are exploring different ways of simplifying the process of application for membership. Some meetings recommend an old Quaker process known as meeting for clearness. This is a process whereby if you wish to apply for membership, you can meet with members of your meeting and talk through what membership might mean to you in an atmosphere of worship. The important thing is that there be time for a gentle reflection on what membership might mean and to allow you to gain a wider insight into the life of the Society.

If you decide to join, even if you do not have a meeting for clearness, the best thing is to discuss this decision with one or two members of your home meeting. Then you send a letter to the Clerk of the Monthly Meeting containing a few details about the contacts you have with the local Meeting. The letter will go to a session of Monthly Meeting which will appoint two Quakers to visit you. One of these visitors will be known to you from the local Meeting, the other will usually come from another Meeting. The basic idea behind this visit is to give you the opportunity of asking questions in a relaxed and informal atmosphere, to find out whether you will feel at home among Quakers, and whether you are committed to basic Quaker attitudes. Several enquirers have told me that they felt they were going to be tested, but in fact they enjoyed the experience of an informal conversation in their own home. Of course we are all afraid of rejection. Most people are accepted, but if it is felt that the applicant really has too little experience of Meeting, or that his or her attitudes are really at odds with Friends then the applicant is usually asked to wait and apply again later after having had more experience of the ways of Quakers. This is not a matter of being rejected, more a matter of honesty and an understanding of the nature of commitment.

The visitors then go back to Monthly Meeting and tell the Friends there about their discussion. Of course confidentiality is respected. There is no welcoming ceremony as such for the new member but the Meeting often expresses its pleasure in a very real and delighted way.

Because Quakers are such a diverse bunch of people, there is no attempt to make anyone conform. Indeed Quakers seem temperamentally nonconformist. On the other hand of course, there is always the danger of institutionalism in any group which has members and a structure. This is a very human weakness, but for all the talk of the smallness of the Society, its committees and its peculiar meetings, it remains a vital force which still says what always needs to be said: there is a power of love that overcomes everything and that lives in the hearts of all human beings. This power has had its human counterpart in the life of Jesus of Nazareth and is seen in the lives of many people of all religions and of none. It is alive in each one of us; it can demand from us a deep commitment, and can challenge the way we live, treat others and care for our planet. It is a source of joy and freedom as it reveals to us our divine potential. Above all, it empowers us as we respond to it in worship. The light that illuminates us is the light that illuminates all of creation. It is the light that is eternally shining.

REFERENCES

1   Elizabeth Kübler-Ross, *Death, the Final Stage of Growth.*
    Englewood Cliffs, NJ, USA: Prentice Hall, 1975, p. 164
2   William Penn, *A Collection of the Works of William Penn.*
    London, 1726, II, p. 781
3   George Fox, *The Journal of George Fox* ed J. L. Nickalls.
    London: Cambridge University Press, 1952; London Yearly
    Meeting, rpt. 1975 p. 19
4   Elie Wiesel, *Night* trs. S. Rodway. Harmondsworth, Middx:
    Penguin Books, 1981
5   Isaac Penington, *The Light Within and Selected Writings of
    Isaac Penington.* Philadelphia, PA, USA: Tract Association
    of Friends, n.d. p. 2
6   Lewis Benson, *George Fox's Message is Relevant Today.*
    New Foundation Publication 2, 1977
7   Robert Barclay, *Apology.* Proposition 10, section 2. London
    edn., 1678, pp. 181–2
8   Ibid
9   *Advices & Queries*, Britain Yearly Meeting, rpt. 2000.
    Section 1
10 Caroline Stephen, *Quaker Strongholds.* Friends Home
    Service Committee, 1908, rpt. 1966, p. 8
11 Thomas Kelly, *The Gathered Meeting.* London: Friends
    Home Service Committee, 1944, p. 12; also *Reality of the
    Spiritual World and the Gathered Meeting.* London:
    Friends Home Service Committee, 1965, p. 49
12 John Punshon, *Portrait in Grey.* London: Quaker Home
    Service, 1984, p. 37
13 Rufus M. Jones, *The Flowering of Mysticism.* New York,
    USA: Macmillan, 1939, p. 251

14   Thomas Ellwood, *History of the Life of Thomas
      Ellwood…Written by His Own Hand* (1714) ed. C. G. Crump.
      London: Methuen, 1900, pp. 23–4

15   John Woolman, 'A Plea for the Poor' quoted in *The Wisdom
      of John Woolman* by Reginald Reynolds. Quaker Home
      Service, 1948, rpt. 1988, p. 142

16   *Advices & Queries*, op. cit., p. 15

17   George Fox, *Journal*, op. cit., p. 65

18   Ibid, pp. 399–400

19   *Advices & Queries*, op. cit., p. 20

20   George H. Gorman, *Introducing Quakers*. London: Quaker
      Home Service, 1969, last revised rpt. 1981, p. 72

FURTHER READING

Advices & Queries, Britain Yearly Meeting, rpt. 2000.
Quaker faith & practice, Britain Yearly Meeting, rpt. 1999.
Yours in Friendship, Richard Allen, QHS, 1995.
Listening to the Light, Jim Pym, Rider, 1999.

HISTORY
British Quakers 1647–1997, Alistair Heron, Curlew Graphics, rpt.1999.
The Journal of George Fox, editor John Nickalls, Philadelphia Yearly Meeting, rpt. 1997.
Portrait in Grey: a short history of the Quakers, John Punshon, Quaker Books, rev. rpt. 2001.
Quakers in Britain – a century of change 1895–1995, Alistair Heron, Curlew Graphics, 1995.
Truth of the Heart, an anthology of George Fox, Rex Ambler, Quaker Books, 2001.

WORSHIP & PRAYER
The Amazing Fact of Quaker Worship, George Gorman, QHS, 1993.
God is Silence, Pierre Lacout, Quaker Books, rpt. 2001.
Nourishing the Spiritual Life, Paul A. Lacey, QHS, 1999.
Prayer and Worship, Douglas V. Steere, Friends United Press, 1998.
Paths of the Spirit, meditations for a journey, compiled by Harvey Gillman, QHS, 1998.
Silence and Speech, Richard Allen, QHS, 1993.

THE BIBLE
Is the Bible Important Today? If so, why? Kenneth Lawton, Joseph Pickvance and John Walters, QHS, 1995.
Twenty Questions About Jesus, John Lampen, QHS, rpt. 1994.

CHILDREN & YOUNG PEOPLE

Good Friends, Judith Baresel, Quaker Books, 2002.

The Peace Kit: everyday peacemaking for young people, John Lampen, QHS, 1992.

A Portrait of Friends – an introduction to the Quakers for young people, Harvey Gillman, QHS, 1993.

QUAKER WORK & WITNESS

The Claims of Conscience, Cecil Evans, QHS, 1996.

Peace in the Power and the Light, David Lonsdale, QHS, 1988.

Peace is a Process, Sydney D. Bailey, QHS and Woodbrooke College, 1993.

Quaker Encounters: A study of two centuries of Quaker activity in the relief of suffering caused by war or natural calamity, Ormerod Greenwood, Sessions, 1975–1978. In three volumes: *Friends and Relief, Vines on the Mountain* and *Whispers of Truth.*

SOCIAL RESPONSIBILITY

Beyond the Spirit of the Age, Jonathan Dale, QHS, 1996.

Faith in Action, Quaker social testimony, Jonathan Dale and others, QHS, 2000.

Forgiving Justice, a Quaker vision for criminal justice, Tim Newell, QHS, 2000.

MODERN QUAKERS

A Faith to Call our Own, Alex Wildwood, QHS, 1999.

Pictorial Guide to the Quaker Tapestry, Quaker Tapestry Scheme, 1998.

The Way Out is the Way In: a Quaker's pilgrimage, Damaris Parker-Rhodes, QHS, 1985.

Who do we think we are? – Young Friends' Commitment and Belonging, QHS, 1998.

THEOLOGY & DOCTRINE
A Certain Kind of Perfection, Margery Post Abbott, Pendle Hill, 1997.
To Lima with Love: the response of the Religious Society of Friends in Great Britain to the World Council of Churches' document 'Baptism, Eucharist and Ministry', Committee on Christian Relationships, QHS, 1987.
Previous Convictions, Christine Trevett, QHS, 1997.
Testimony & Tradition, John Punshon, QHS, 1990.
This I Affirm, QHS, rpt. 2000.

QUAKER ORGANISATION
Beyond Majority Rule: voteless decisions in the Religious Society of Friends, Michael Sheeran SJ, Philadelphia Yearly Meeting, 1983.
Moving into Membership, Committee for Eldership and Oversight, Quaker Books, 2001.

These are some of a wide range of Quaker books which, together with other books on peace, social issues and religion in general, are available from: Quaker Bookshop, Friends House, 173 Euston Road, London NW1 2BJ. Telephone 020 7663 1030 – catalogues available. Email: bookshop@quaker.org.uk
Open Monday–Friday 10–5, occasional Saturdays – ring for details.

For further information about national Quaker work, contact Friends House on 020 7663 1016, website: www.quaker.org.uk

For information on Friends abroad, contact the Friends World Committee for Consultation on 020 7388 0497 or email world@fwcc.quaker.org

The main three Quaker Journals are: *The Friend* (weekly), *Quaker monthly* and *The Friends' Quarterly*. These are all obtainable at the Bookshop.

INDEX